CW00321380

Auschwitz
A Mother's Story

Auschwitz
A Mother's Story

How I fought to survive
and see my daughter again

ROSA DE WINTER-LEVY

monoray

Originally published by Alfabet Uitgevers, The Netherlands, in 2023.
This edition published in Great Britain in 2024 by Monoray, an imprint of
Octopus Publishing Group Ltd
Carmelite House
50 Victoria Embankment
London EC4Y 0DZ
www.octopusbooks.co.uk

An Hachette UK Company
www.hachette.co.uk

© First published by Alfabet Uitgevers, The Netherlands in 2023
Translation Copyright © Octopus Publishing Group 2024

Distributed in the US by
Hachette Book Group
1290 Avenue of the Americas
4th and 5th Floors
New York, NY 10104

Distributed in Canada by
Canadian Manda Group
664 Annette St.
Toronto, Ontario, Canada M6S 2C8

All rights reserved. No part of this work may be reproduced or utilized in any form
or by any means, electronic or mechanical, including photocopying, recording
or by any information storage and retrieval system, without the prior written
permission of the publisher.

Translated from the Dutch by Liz Waters

ISBN 978-1-80096-230-9

A CIP catalogue record for this book is available from the British Library.

Printed and bound in Great Britain.

Typeset in 11/18pt Plantin MT Pro by Jouve (UK), Milton Keynes

1 3 5 7 9 10 8 6 4 2

This FSC® label means that materials used
for the product have been responsibly sourced.

This monoray book was crafted and published by Jake Lingwooed, Mala Sanghera-
Warren, Alex Stetter, Liz Waters, Mel Four and Katherine Hockley

Contents

About the authors

Rosa de Winter-Levy was born in Gelsenkirchen, Germany in 1905, to a Dutch father and a German mother. At the age of 19, after the deaths of both her parents, she moved to the Netherlands, where she married Emanuel de Winter (1889–1944). In 1928, the couple welcomed a daughter, Judy. After the Second World War, Rosa lived once again in the Netherlands. She died in 1985.

Ronit Palache (b. 1984) is a Dutch journalist and author.

Rosa with her husband Emanuel and daughter Judy

Introduction

'It has always been my wish, and in my deepest misery I resolved, should I withstand the suffering, to make known to the world my experiences in the concentration camp Birkenau at Auschwitz in Poland.' This is how Rosa de Winter-Levy begins her testimony.

The NIOD Institute for War, Holocaust and Genocide Studies in Amsterdam holds more than 2,200 wartime diaries, memoirs and other unpublished first-hand accounts.[1] Every week, new, previously unknown documents are added to its collection, donated by family members who no longer wish to keep them, or who regard them as so important that they want to see them preserved at a central location. Sometimes they are given to national memorial centres in the Netherlands such as Camp Vught or Camp Westerbork, sometimes to local resistance museums and sometimes to the website *Het geheugen van Nederland* (The Memory of the Netherlands).[2] We cannot know precisely how many diaries and other personal accounts were written between 1940 and 1945, but anxious and desperate questions such as 'What awaits us now?', 'Are we going to survive this?' and 'Will we ever see each other again?' must have been committed to paper on countless occasions. They make an impression every time, because behind each of them stands an individual, a unique person with a specific past. None of their written reactions, however similar they may seem, can even begin to convey to readers the depth of feeling experienced by the victims.

'Nobody who hasn't experienced it can understand what this means for us,' wrote Rosa de Winter-Levy in the 'pamphlet' *Aan de gaskamer ontsnapt! Het Satanswerk van de S.S. (Escaped from the gas chamber! The satanic work of the S.S.)*, which was published shortly after the war, in September 1945, by Uitgeversmaatschappij C. Misset, a publishing company in the province of Gelderland. This document, probably created by a journalist at the

newspaper *de Gelderlander*,[3] is one of the few testimonies
published that year.[4] It is a forty-six-page account of the
author's time in hiding in Gelderland and as a prisoner
in Westerbork and Auschwitz-Birkenau.

Escaped from the gas chamber!, retitled *Auschwitz – A
Mother's Story* for this edition, is not a diary, as the
experiences described in it were not noted down daily
during the period in which they took place – that being
the narrow definition with which a diary would have
to comply. But these are certainly autobiographical
recollections. Furthermore, the descriptions are mostly
so accurate and detailed (including dates and locations)
that they do justice to experiences and feelings as stored
in the memory, not least because they were committed
to paper and actually published so soon after the end
of the war.[5] Yet memory is always treacherous, as
becomes clear after reading both Rosa de Winter's
account of events and the interviews that she gave later
(in some cases decades after its publication). Depending
on how much time passes between the experience
and its description in retrospect, memories can be
distorted, coloured or framed by a new language of
readily available clichés. In subsequent phases of a life,

a different emphasis can come to be placed on certain memories, and things may be forgotten for the sake of self-preservation.[6]

Nevertheless, these and all kinds of other complex issues relating to experiences in the past and the presumed facts about them hardly detract from the importance of this form of written heritage. Or, as the interviewer of de Winter's daughter Judy on behalf of the Anne Frank Foundation concludes, 'One memory may be a little different from another, but that is not to say that one is true and the other untrue.'[7] Testimony of this sort contributes to the collective memory and conveys – if in some cases only in very small part – the terrible circumstances in which people could find themselves as a result of the acts or omissions of others. For their readers or surviving relatives, for historians or people who develop an interest, such personal documents are of inestimable value. The fact that experiences have been shared and written down enables us to gain a clearer view of once extant, already repeated and potentially repeatable realities.

The testimony of Rosa de Winter is no exception. She tells us in a matter-of-fact style, and at the same time in no uncertain terms, what happened to her, to her husband Emanuel and daughter Judy (called Hetty in de Winter's account), to her relatives and to others during the Second World War, especially in the Auschwitz extermination camp. The document is primarily descriptive, an account of what happened in the camp, an indictment of 'the vassals, of members of the NSB and the German tyrant's *Landwacht*, who were complicit in subjecting so many to the cruellest of tortures'.[8] It is an attempt to depict what has time and again been called unimaginable: people's terror of the unknown fate that awaited them, their uncertainty and later certainty as to what those smoking chimneys signified, how for utterly inexplicable reasons they had to stand naked for hours at roll call, the arbitrariness of their treatment by the brutes in charge, the good fortune of occasionally being able to swap a piece of clothing for some bread and turnip, or vice versa, the horrific separation from loved ones, the disease, the lice, the fear, cold, hunger, exhaustion, callousness and death.

'Nobody who hasn't experienced it can understand what this means for us.' It is the sentence that opens the chapter 'On a transport to the east', on page 55. Yet that is precisely what historians and writers have tried to do in their countless studies and books, anthologies and analyses, poems and plays, films and documentaries. What happened there? What can we understand about it? What does it say about us, about the human species? Every Dutch person will be familiar with the words *Nooit meer Auschwitz* (Never again Auschwitz), which form part of the monument created by writer and artist Jan Wolkers in Amsterdam in 1977 – an invocatory form of words that has not prevented people elsewhere in the world from being murdered or dehumanized right up to the present day. Because in essence that is what Auschwitz was all about: the murder and dehumanization of Jews, of our fellow human beings.

Among them was survivor Rosa de Winter-Levy, reduced during her time in Auschwitz to number A25250. Her daughter Judy was given the next number in the sequence. This apparently random combination of letters and figures remained tattooed on Judy's lower left arm for the rest of her life. In a conversation with a researcher at the Anne Frank Foundation, she said that after the war a doctor who examined her wanted to remove the tattoo: 'I'll do that in a jiffy.'[9] But Judy refused. 'It doesn't trouble me,' she said. In reality she was bewildered by the silence about everything that had happened, even on the part of the person treating her. Nothing was asked. Nobody received appropriate care.[10]

* * *

'Röschen' (Rosa)

Rosa Levy was born on 9 June 1905 in Gelsenkirchen, Germany, the fifth child of liberal Jewish parents: cattle dealer Jonas Levi from Doetinchem, in the Dutch province of Gelderland, and Adelheid Hamberg from Breuna, near the city of Kassel in Germany. Jonas died of the Spanish flu twelve years after Rosa was born, and her mother was probably seriously ill by then too. In July of that year, Rosa was sent to Doetinchem, where she was entrusted to the safe keeping of three aunts who ran a sewing workshop there.[11] Rosa was a resident of Doetinchem for two years, but in 1919 she returned to Germany to join her brother and sisters and finish secondary school. Her mother died on 3 March 1920. Rosa's brother Moritz and sister Helene died young, on

The Levy children, *c*.1919. Top, from left to right: Julie (b.1898), Ella (b.1901), Moritz (b.1894). Bottom: Rosa (b.1905) and Helene (b.1893).

9 August 1919 and 1 February 1922 respectively, for reasons that remain unclear.

After leaving school, Rosa took a job in a clothing shop in Essen and then moved to the Netherlands permanently at the age of nineteen. She worked as a saleswoman at the Maison de Bonneterie department store in The Hague before marrying Emanuel (Manus) de Winter in 1927. A year after their wedding, by which time the young couple had moved to Zutphen in the province of Gelderland, their daughter Judy was born, on 27 October 1928. Manus ran a butcher's shop along with his brothers Max and Ferdinand, and Rosa regularly worked there at the till.

Judy attended a state school. Being Jewish played no appreciable role in the lives of the de Winters, but as the Nazi race laws started to encroach upon them, Judy was obliged to attend the Jewish high school in Arnhem and was given a special permit to travel there. Under German occupation, the authorities forced Jews to make more and more sacrifices by the day, to relinquish bit by bit everything that gave shape to their everyday lives.

By 1943 normal life was a distant memory, but the

family, with daughter Judy now aged fourteen, was still intact. That is the situation at the start of Rosa de Winter-Levy's story. 'The three of us are still in our own home. For how much longer? The laws and regulations decreed by the Germans follow each other in quick succession. Every day brings new worries; we live under great stress. Terrible. The ring around the little freedom left to us grows tighter and tighter. This is the final phase; we can feel it coming.'

★ ★ ★

Their prediction proved correct. Rosa and her husband decided not to go voluntarily to Vught, the camp to which Jews were ordered to report, but instead went into hiding in April 1943 at the home of farmer Lettink and his family (she calls them 'the E. family' in her published account) in Varsseveld. They had come into contact with the Lettinks through Rosa's sister Ella, who had been living in Varsseveld since 1922, and her brother-in-law Leys, who was a cattle dealer. Through his job, Leys knew exactly which people in the Gelderland village were still to be trusted.

Rosa, Emanuel and Judy had a good time with the Lettinks, despite the daily grind of life in hiding.[12]

Rosa's engagement photograph, 1927

Rosa with Judy in the pram on Nieuwstad in Zutphen,
The Netherlands, *c*.1929

Although the farming family was poor, the de Winters were not asked to pay for their accommodation, only for food. When it was cold, Mrs Lettink let Rosa and her daughter sleep in her bed to get warm. But then disaster struck. After a relatively uneventful stay lasting 464 days, they were betrayed in the night of 16–17 July 1944, probably by a member of the SS who was spying in the area.[13]

According to Ernst Schnabel's *Spur eines Kindes* (published in English as *The Footsteps of Anne Frank*), a 1958 biography of Anne Frank that was based on documentary evidence and accounts by surviving witnesses, the couple and their daughter were taken to a police station in Arnhem. From Rosa's account and a conversation between Judy and the Anne Frank Foundation many years later, it emerges that they were held in Velp, a village on the edge of the city. There Rosa refused to divulge the names of others who had gone into hiding. 'Even if you shoot me dead, I don't know anyone anywhere around here.'[14] This is characteristic of the resilience she showed both during and after the war. Judy recalled being impressed at that moment: 'My mother gave nothing away.'[15]

After a week at the police station, the three of them were put on a train to Westerbork, along with twenty-two other people.[16] A month later, Rosa met Anne Frank at the camp, along with the other former inhabitants of the secret annex in Amsterdam. She was glad that the Franks, with whom she became friends, had a daughter of Judy's age with them. Rosa talked about Anne mainly in interviews conducted after the publication of her own testimony, when Anne Frank had already become a worldwide symbol of the persecution of the Jews. She was prompted to do so by questions from interviewers such as Koos Postema (of *Achter het Nieuws*, a current affairs television show), who tended to focus on the part the Franks had played in Rosa de Winter-Levy's wartime story. In her own book, Rosa mentions only Edith, Anne's mother. Nevertheless, from later accounts it is clear that she retained vivid memories of Anne. In a conversation with Ernst Schnabel she said, for instance, 'Perhaps I couldn't say that her eyes shone. But they had a warm glow, you know what I mean? And she was so free in her movements, and in her way of looking, that I wondered, "Is she actually happy, then?" She *was* happy in Westerbork, although that's almost impossible to understand, because we didn't have a good life in the camp. We "criminal Jews", who had been caught at the places where we'd gone into in hiding, were treated even more harshly than the others. [. . .] Anne could still smile, whereas I kept asking myself: Will they send us to Poland? Will we get out of this alive?'[17]

Rosa also recalled that when Anne was ill, Otto came to sit with his daughter in Westerbork and spent hours telling her stories. In the camp Anne proved herself to be an extremely caring person. Although she was the youngest, it was she who shared out bread and unexpectedly presented Rosa with a pair of men's long trousers. When at one point Rosa almost fainted with thirst, Anne turned up with a cup of hot coffee. It was a mystery how she had managed that in such circumstances. 'Anne was defenceless to the last,' Rosa said. She still had tears in her eyes when the rest of us could no longer cry.[18] Rosa told the coffee anecdote slightly differently in an interview in the newspaper *Het Vrije Volk* of 28 May 1964, and on the television programme *Achter het Nieuws* that same year. It is now Judy for whom Anne conjures up coffee: 'We'd been at roll call with our tongues sticking out of our mouths, simply to catch the raindrops or snowflakes, because we were given hardly anything to drink. By then our intestines were quite dehydrated. But one night when my daughter was delirious with fever, Anne managed to get hold of a cup of black coffee. She'd done her very best to help someone. Which is truly admirable in a child of that age.'[19] It is another example of how details may vary here and there in the anecdotes that Rosa related.

The de Winters were with the Franks on 2 September 1944 when they were all put on a transport to the east – to Auschwitz, as it turned out.[20] Shortly before their departure from Westerbork, Rosa wrote another letter to her family in Varsseveld: 'Tomorrow, 3 September, we're going on a transport. We don't yet know where to, but it will be to the east. We are full of courage and still healthy and will do our best to get through it. We're in a dreadful plight here. Give our greetings and this letter to Elsje and Lammert especially; we long to see them again and will have to fight for that. [. . .] Don't send any more things to us here, we'll come and fetch them from you later. Thanks for everything. Greetings and kisses, especially to my family.'[21] She signed the letter 'Ma, Ro, Ju' – *Ma* stands for Manus, *Ro* for Rosa, *Ju* for Judy.

During that journey, Rosa's husband seems to have had little confidence that things would turn out well for them. In the train, Manus expressed to his wife his gratitude for the life they had led together, but Rosa did not want to listen. 'What do you mean by that? We're going to live, aren't we?'[22] Rosa wanted only one thing: to survive. That lust for life can be read between the lines again and again, sometimes expressed in so many words: 'I don't want to die, I tell Jo. I'm still young and love life.'[23]

But the couple's life together ends abruptly when they arrive at the death camp, where men and women are brutally separated. Judy talked about that later. 'When you got out of that train, the first thing was tremendous screaming. Inconceivable. Truly terrible. [. . .] My father was in that group of men and I looked back, I remember that. I waved. "Stay strong," I said. Something like that. Or "Chin up". One of those things. And that was it.'[24] In her book, Rosa writes of the moment when she saw her 55-year-old husband for the last time: 'My husband glances at me sorrowfully, a look I will never forget. It's just a brief moment. He's herded away from me without a parting word.' Ernst Schnabel quotes her as saying it was 'as if he suddenly disappeared from the face of the earth'.[25]

Until Judy's birthday on 27 October 1944, mother and daughter managed to stay together under increasingly difficult circumstances. But then they were separated. Judy was sent to a munitions factory in Chrastava, in the Sudetenland.[26] Anne and Margot Frank were not able to go with her, because Anne had scabies and Margot volunteered to stay behind with her sister.[27] They left Auschwitz three days later nevertheless, but not for the same destination as Judy. Instead they were transferred to Bergen-Belsen. Rosa remembered their mother's despair. 'Edith cried out: The children, oh god.'[28]

Once again, the memories recorded in her published account differ in places from how Rosa later described her time in the camp without her daughter. This book includes passages about her 'camp friend' Jo and how she dies in Rosa's arms. Years later, in her interview with Koos Postema and six years before that in a conversation with Ernst Schnabel for the book *Spur eines Kindes*, Rosa said that it was Edith she came upon again in the infirmary block and who died in her arms on 6 January 1945.[29] 'I wanted desperately to stay alive, but eventually I got sick. I came into the *Ambulanz*, the clinic, and there saw Mrs Frank. I went to lie next to her. She was very weak and no longer eating. She was barely conscious. She stashed everything she was given to eat under her blanket. She said she was keeping it for her husband because he needed it so badly, and so the bread rotted in her bed.[30] I don't know whether she was so weak because she wasn't eating or whether she was too weak to eat. You could no longer tell by looking at her. I watched her die, without a murmur. I thought, "Now you'll die yourself, too." '[31]

But Rosa went on living. When on 27 January 1945 the Russians liberated Auschwitz, she was still in the infirmary at Birkenau. She ignored the order to leave the camp on a forced march. There, in a camp abandoned by the Germans, with its well-stocked store cupboards, she remained until 19 March, regaining her strength. She still knew nothing of the fate of her husband and daughter. After a long journey with 150 other survivors, Rosa arrived in Odessa. They travelled there via Katowice, where Rosa recognized Otto Frank and informed him of his wife's death: 'Mr Frank didn't move when I told him. I looked at him but he turned away and then he did move. I no longer know exactly what kind of movement it was, but I believe he laid his head on the table.'[32] Among the people who travelled with her were fifteen-year-old Eva Geiringer and Eva's mother Fritzi Geiringer-Markovits, who became Otto's wife after the war. Rosa had got to know Fritzi in Auschwitz.

Before the war, Fritzi and Eva were part of a family of four that lived opposite the Franks on the Merwedeplein in Amsterdam. When I spoke to Eva (by then Eva Schloss) by telephone, she told me how sad and despairing Rosa (whom she called Rootje) was during their time in Odessa. 'The whole day long she wondered where her daughter could be, whether she was still alive. She wasn't really jealous, but she kept looking at my mother and me. The comfort we had in each other, waiting for news about my father Erich and brother Heinz, was hard for her to bear. She was alone all the time and had no idea what had happened to her husband and daughter.'

When the war in Europe ended on 8 May, they travelled together from Odessa on a ship called the *Monowai*, across the Black Sea and then on to Marseille. There Rosa wrote a letter to her sister and brother-in-law in Varsseveld. She was convinced they had survived. 'The miracle has happened. I've been saved and am healthy. Manus was taken from me back in September on our arrival, and I've never heard anything further from him. Judy was sent to work in Germany on 27 October and I don't know whether she's still alive. [. . .] Please pass on this message to the whole family and try to see whether you can find Manus + Judy.'[33] From Marseille they were supposed to travel by train straight to Holland, but because of a damaged bridge they got no further than Vlodrop near Roermond, in the southern Dutch province of Limburg, where they arrived on 31 May and stayed overnight in a monastery called St. Ludwig Klooster. There, in Limburg, Rootje was miraculously reunited with her daughter. It is where her account ends.

* * *

'The reunion of mother and daughter had a great impact on the other survivors,' Eva told me. 'Every day, people from the camps were arriving. Rootje went to the station each time, with high hopes, to see whether her daughter was among the passengers. One day we heard loud cries and saw Rootje deliriously happy with a girl on her arm. "My daughter! My daughter!" she kept shouting. "I've found Judy." She kissed and hugged her. It was such an unbelievably beautiful moment for every one of us. We were so happy for her. We had each other, but until then she'd been alone all the time. It gave everyone hope, including Otto, who was waiting for his daughters. When the bridge was finally repaired, we left for Holland at last. We decided there and then to remain friends.'

Rosa immediately wrote from Limburg to her sister and brother-in-law in Varsseveld. She had already written to them from Marseille, but now she could give them the joyful news that she had found her daughter. 'I arrived here on a big transport from Odessa and an indescribable miracle has happened. I met Judy here, who has come from the Sudetenland. She wasn't liberated until 8 May, she's still weak and thin and I've been free for four months and am plump and healthy. Manus hasn't been found yet. We'll get ourselves home as quickly as possible. We're very, very happy and hoping to see you soon. I long for you deeply and have oh, so much to tell you. We still don't know when we'll be arriving and I'll write to you then. Lots of loving greetings, your Röschen.'[34]

Since other people were living in the prewar family home in Zutphen, on their return to the Netherlands Rosa and Judy had no option but to move into Ella's house in Varsseveld. Rosa's sister had indeed survived the war. Severely weakened, they gradually recovered from 'experiencing all these things'.[35] It was there that Rosa's wartime memories were written down by a journalist. After a few months, mother and daughter were able to return to the house in Zutphen, although the upper floor was still occupied by another homeless family.

It was not long before Rosa rolled up her sleeves and went to live above a drapery shop in Apeldoorn called 't Stoffenhuis, where she had taken a job. The business, established in 1937, belonged to Philip Lezer, husband of the daughter of Emanuel's brother. It was Lezer who asked Rosa to take over the management of the shop when it reopened in 1947. Judy meanwhile finished secondary school, qualified as a pharmacy assistant and worked for a short time at a pharmacy in Apeldoorn. In 1951 she visited her cousin Jetty and family in Israel, where she seems to have been very happy. A letter to Rosa from Jetty's husband David suggests that Judy felt more at home there than in the Netherlands and wanted to investigate opportunities to stay in Israel. Nevertheless, 'She is of the opinion that she definitely doesn't want to do anything that would not give you a chance to stay with her [. . .].'[36]

The powerful emotions evoked in Rosa at the thought of once more being separated from her daughter become clear again later, in the interview that Judy gave to the Anne Frank Foundation. 'The first portents [of psychiatric problems] were a sense of abandonment and that kind of thing. A fear that I would leave. She kept getting it into her head [. . .] that I'd go somewhere without letting her know, which is really how it all started.'[37] According to her son Marcel Salomon, Judy did indeed decide to return to the Netherlands for that reason. He believes it is not entirely by chance that less than a year later – by which time she was living in Amsterdam – she became engaged to his future father, Henk Salomon, a young man who had initially proposed to Eva Geiringer. 'I couldn't love anyone yet, at that time,' Eva told me. 'My father, yes, but he was no longer there. I was too damaged for such feelings, but I liked Henk very much and he wanted to marry me. I wanted children no matter what. That became my goal in life. At the same time another boy, an Israeli, asked for my hand. I turned to my mother for advice. In her estimation, there was a lot I could learn from the Israeli and she thought Henk was too shallow. My grandmother proposed introducing Henk to Rootje's daughter Judy, who had just returned from Israel. So we did. During a dinner on the Merwedeplein, where my mother and I had returned after the war, they clicked. I married Zvi, my Israeli, and Judy got engaged to Henk. My mother had been right.'[38]

Rosa, Fritzi and Otto saw a lot of each other. 'After Otto married my mother, they regularly asked Rootje to join them on holiday in Switzerland. She never remarried and sometimes seemed rather lonely, so she enjoyed those trips.' Marcel and Henriette, Judy's children, who are interviewed at the end of this book about their memories of their mother and grandmother, fondly remember their meetings with Otto and Fritzi.

Marcel was born in 1957 in Amstelveen, just outside Amsterdam. Rosa moved there three years after he was born to be closer to her daughter and the young family. Henriette was born in 1965. In Amstelveen,

Rosa once again proved a hard worker. She took another job in the fashion trade, this time at a clothes shop called Princesse, and made herself useful to the Jewish organization WIZO (Women's International Zionist Organization). Jewish women regularly gathered in her house on the Meander, to collect clothes for the cause.

In 1964, Rosa gave several interviews during the build-up to the Auschwitz trials, in which, after long hesitation, she had decided to participate. Fritz Bauer, the chief prosecutor, invited her to Frankfurt to testify. It was the first time since the war that she had been back to Germany and she found that difficult. 'It has been very hard for me to make that decision. Not because I want to forget, but because I will have to experience again the unhappiest months of my life. I don't know whether I can cope with the emotions. But I'll have to. I must tell the stories of all those people who fought a losing battle with such dignity.'[39]

'Her testimony is not specifically targeted at one or more former Nazis who must be held to account for the indescribable misery they caused,' the article goes on. 'It should be seen far more as testimony in the general sense, as a warning, intended for the younger generation

—28—

in particular, for whom the Second World War does not evoke terrifying memories. As a convincing appeal for such a thing never to happen again.'

In another of her interviews, with *Het Vrije Volk*, Rosa says that at night she sometimes screams in her sleep and that 'the thin copper tubes of the lamp on her ceiling suddenly remind her of the thin pipes of the "showers" in the gas chambers of Auschwitz'. She had narrowly escaped those showers by pure chance: 'We were driven inside for a hot bath. It was crazy. Heavily armed SS men stood at the door. We'd been given a towel and a piece of soap. A hot bath at last! But no water came out of those narrow pipes. After a long wait we had to go out again, still dirty. Later we heard there had been some kind of problem with the gas supply.'[40]

In the interview with Koos Postema mentioned above, she even talked about having hallucinations that confronted her with everything she had experienced. 'You lie awake for hours. But you can't complain, because that's just how it is. You can't trouble your neighbours about it, or people close to you, or your family. You have to keep going. That's my duty. And I make the best of it.'[41]

Rosa told Ernst Schnabel, whom she describes as animated, handsome and friendly, 'You just have to get through it somehow.' It is the same tone as we find in her published account. She describes the terrible conditions in the camp at length and in detail, while saying almost nothing about how much she missed her husband and daughter or about other emotions. She was concentrating on trying to survive and care for the friends she had made in the camp. It seemed impossible to look beyond the present moment in such circumstances. Eva, however, remembered the fears of her parents' friends after the war. 'Rootje did reasonably well at first, but later that changed and she suddenly didn't want to go out with us any more and became frightened. She had delusions that eventually led to her being admitted to an institution. It was a terrible thing to see.'[42]

Judy describes her mother in those final years as like 'an elastic band that suddenly snaps'.[43] In a book by Ryan M. Cooper, *We Never Said Goodbye: Memories of Otto Frank*, she is quoted as saying that towards the end of her life her mother regularly woke at night, sometimes running through the house and screaming in fear of gas. In that period she was admitted to a Jewish mental health institution called Sinai. It was there that she died on 16 September 1985, at the age of eighty. Her daughter Judy died on 11 August 2019.

* * *

Following the approach of the Jewish writer Elie Wiesel (1928–2016), the testimony of Rosa de Winter-Levy makes witnesses of us all.[44] When I began writing this introduction, I was asked what sets her book apart from other wartime testimonies. 'Nothing,' I said. Yet this is no ordinary story. None of the supposedly similar stories are ordinary stories, because every one of them, each in its own unique way, tells of unique people who, for no legitimate reason, were tormented to the point that it determined the entire course of their lives and to some extent shaped the generation or generations that came after them. Rosa de Winter-Levy's story, her far from ordinary story, the story of her murdered husband Emanuel, of her daughter Judy, whom she found again, and the story her grandchildren tell at the end of this book give us once again an opportunity to learn from those 2,200 testimonies held by the NIOD, to which more are added every week, what human beings are capable of doing to each other and how, despite such horrors, people are still determined to live. So they carry on, have children, keep going, retain their lust for life, sometimes snap like elastic bands and yet are able to pass on testimony. Rosa de Winter-Levy was probably right when she wrote that we cannot imagine what she describes because we have not experienced it ourselves, but because of her openness and courage, her storytelling abilities and her memory, we come another step closer. However sad that may be, for history and our historical awareness it is indispensable.

Ronit Palache

January 2023

Rosa with her daughter Judy, *c.*1940

In Birkenau – A Testimony

by Rosa de Winter-Levy

Foreword

Dear reader

*It has always been my wish, and in my deepest
misery I resolved, should I withstand the suffering,
to make known to the world my experiences in
the concentration camp Birkenau at Auschwitz
in Poland. This little book must also serve as an
indictment of the vassals, members of the NSB[1]
and of the German tyrant's Landwacht,[2] who were
complicit in subjecting so many to the cruellest of
tortures. Yet I will try, although it was terrible, to
express myself in the gentlest possible terms and to
paint an accurate picture for you, dear reader, of the
barbarism under which I was imprisoned for several*

months. I also want to describe how, despite the fact that my life had already been written off, I was saved and found my daughter again, who had been torn from me by the brutes.

After I was freed by the Russians on 27 January 1945, we were reunited at Vlodrop on 31 May 1945. What I have written gives an accurate impression of the mistreatment of the prisoners in the Birkenau camp. It is a truthful depiction.

Zutphen, 1 September 1945
Rosa de Winter-Levy

Rosa, Judy and Emanuel, 1940

It's March 1943. The three of us are still in our own home. For how much longer? The laws and regulations decreed by the Germans follow each other in quick succession. Every day brings new worries; we live under great stress. Terrible. The ring around the little freedom left to us grows tighter and tighter. This is the final phase; we can feel it coming.

On 28 March we read in the newspaper:

Jews in the province of Gelderland must report to Vught by 10 April 1943.

This tells us everything. Too much, in fact. We know what Vught means. Imprisonment, isolation, 'concentration camp'. Family life abruptly ended. Not that, never! Giving ourselves up to the enemy without a fight, last of all that! Our plan is ready; we're going into hiding. We have only twelve days left in our own home. Forced to say farewell to everything that has become dear to you over the years – it's frightening to have to take such a step into the unknown, to flee like a thief in the night to the village of V. in the Gelderse Achterhoek,[3] where the E. family is prepared to hide us, to try to keep us out of the hands of the cruel occupier, to save us at great risk to themselves.

The final days fly past. We count the hours. Hetty, our daughter, leaves inconspicuously on 7 April. It's the first time she's been away from the place that's sacred to her, the family home. A day later, my husband and I follow. We arrive at the E. family's house in the evening and they greet us with a warmth characteristic of Achterhoekers. We are welcomed into the family circle and all eat the evening gruel together. A brief chat and then we go to bed, tired out by the tension.

A new era dawns; we're in hiding now, our last

chance. Will we get through it? Who knows? We're full of good cheer. Every day, in our attic room, we devise plans for how we'll make our time as productive as possible. We decide that my husband will help in the farmyard, to make the work of Bernhard, the farmer, easier. But he can only do that in the early morning hours. He mustn't be seen. 'People might come by.' My daughter and I knit, sew, read and look after the children. Little Henkie and his sister take our mind off things and give us great pleasure.

Every day brings the same grind. We follow the war reports with enormous interest. *It's going well*, but how much longer now? We hear that the Allies landed in Normandy on 6 June 1944. Our joy is unbounded. It might be over soon! Free again. Things turn out differently. We're no strategists; we have to go on waiting.

> *Wait, wait, with endless complaint,*
> *That can never alleviate the wait.*

Every day we make a mark in our book. There are already 464 of them. It's now Sunday 16 July, a day we spent quietly and calmly. In the evening we talk until late with Bernhard and Drika about how things used to be and about the time to come, when the war is over. We go peacefully to sleep. Around two in the morning I wake up with a start. I can hear something! Oh, it'll just be the cows grazing close to the house. No, there's a crunching on the gravel. A banging on the front door. A loud voice shouts, '*Juden, rauskommen!*' (Jews, come outside!) What shall we do? Seized by fear, we're already out of our beds. We can't get away now, the house is surrounded. Men in green uniforms and members of the *Landwacht* are already on the stairs!

'What's going on?' I ask in a trembling voice.

'We're looking for Jews. Show us your papers.'

We nervously obey the order. Our papers are forged, but sadly they're not up to date. I ask one elderly Landwachter, who judging by his brutal performance seems to be the commander, to let my daughter go. But all my pleas are in vain. She'll have to come with us. Our suitcases are packed, blankets rolled up, and after a sorrowful parting from our dear guardians we're on our way to the town hall in V. Will we ever see them again?

Locked in a cell, it's only at this point that great distress descends upon us. Now it's all over. What awaits us? If only we're allowed to stay together.

After several fearful hours, the lock grinds and two 'gentlemen' walk in. We say, 'Good morning' and are answered with '*Der Kerl muss mit.*' (The guy comes with us.) Hetty and I are left behind, anxious. After a while my husband is brought back in by the *Sicherheitsdienst* (SS intelligence agency). We are searched and our money is taken. Then we're made to get into a small car and driven to Velp. In the SD building each of us, separately, is subjected to a harsh interrogation. One of the men is notably courteous towards me. I'm on my guard. He wants to make an exception of me and my daughter and take us to Theresienstadt, the camp for 'privileged' Jews – as long as I tell him where others are hiding. But I stand firm and say, 'Even if you shoot me dead, I don't know anyone anywhere around here.' He answers indignantly, '*Totschießen tun wir niemand.*' (We don't shoot anyone dead.) 'Well then,' I say, 'you'll take us to the gas chamber.' At that he shouts, '*Die verdammte Lügenpropaganda von England!*' (Those damned propagandist lies from England!) In short, he realizes I'm not going to give anything away, shrugs his shoulders and leaves the room.

In the corridor we come upon my husband. Oh, the sight of the poor man. They've beaten him black and blue; he didn't know anything either. We look into each other's eyes and understand everything immediately.

Back in the car, we're off to the jail in Arnhem, without our luggage, which will apparently be sent on later. A promise that is never kept. Here my husband and I are separated, for the first time in our marriage. In the prison, life isn't too bad at all. My daughter and I are taken to a large cell with ten other women in it, including political prisoners, who greet us warmly.

The food is decent, except that we don't like the sour, dry bread. Twice a day we're allowed some fresh air in a courtyard downstairs, like monkeys in a cage. When the men are in the courtyard, we can see them from our window, my husband among them. He looks up and signals, 'Stay strong; chin up.' Hetty and I savour those wonderful moments until the next day. From our window at the front, we look out on a warehouse where young men are working. We're very eager to hear war reports and one of us has a good idea. On a white cloth she embroiders in big red letters: NEWS? The lads turn out to be made of the right stuff. They understand. The next day we see them hold a large blackboard up to the window and written on it in white chalk is 'ATTACK ON HITLER, REVOLUTION IN GERMANY!' We draw courage from that. Might it perhaps soon be over now?

To Westerbork

A few days later, however, a guard comes in and says with a sad face, 'The Jewish ladies need to be ready this afternoon. There's a transport to Westerbork at three o'clock.' It's like a bolt from the blue. Another parting from several of our roommates.

In the afternoon, twenty-five men and women, in a dejected mood, stand together in the hall. We're counted by SS men and our names are called out, then we get into a bus bound for the province of Drenthe.

On the way there, Hetty sits close to her father, whom she's been missing all this time. At ten in the evening, we see Camp Westerbork far off across the heath. It doesn't look too bad to us – we see some nice wooden houses with gardens in front. But we're not allowed to stay there. We have to walk on further, to the punishment barracks. First we're registered and given a medical examination. Our clothes are taken from us, everything but our underwear, and we're given blue overalls with red backs. The men, who've had their heads shaved, are given blue-and-red caps. Shoes have to be handed in too and we're all given clogs. That's not easy for me, since I've never worn clogs before, but I'll have to get used to them.

The first night on a straw mattress without a blanket, in a barracks with three hundred women, I can't sleep. The next morning a surprise awaits me: I meet my sister with her husband and son. We haven't seen each other for two years and now it's in the midst of all this misery. Julie is very spirited, greeting me with the words, 'Don't cry, it's quite bearable here if you just persevere.' Indeed, that's how it is.

My husband has been taken to the men's barracks, which is close to ours. The next day we're on the list for work and we get the hardest, filthiest work in Westerbork: *Batteries*. It's a special industry, with more than a thousand people working in it. From old batteries that have been smashed to pieces we extract the brown

coal, which is used for the war effort. It's a comfort that
men and women work together here.

At five in the morning we're made to get up and, led
by the *Ordnungsdienst* (police service),[4] we walk to work
in a procession, three people wide. From six to three in
the dust, while the sun is shining outside. We return
from work very dirty, but we're allowed a hot shower
every day and then food.

Here too the food is still decent, although it's a shame
we're no longer permitted to receive parcels because
we're being punished for having gone into hiding.

Our Hetty works at *Cables*, from seven to seven,
another industry for the war effort. It's not difficult
work; separating the copper from the insulation. On
Sundays we don't have to work, but there's gym for the
women in the mornings and an hour of exercise for the
men. Other than that, we're together all day, fortunately.
Hetty has settled in already; she's with other girls and
boys of around fifteen or sixteen. Relations between all
of the campmates are good. Our only hope is that there
will be no more transports. But that hope proves vain.
A large goodwill transport leaves for Theresienstadt in
Czechoslovakia,[5] and my sister and her family are on it.

The 'privileged' set off in good spirits with their luggage. This parting is another of many disappointments. Will we ever see each other again? We're left behind, filled with fear and dread. Everything goes on as before. Work, sleep, catch fleas and eat a little. If only we can just stay together until the war is over. But sadly, on 1 September we're taken from our work by the *Ordnungsdienst* and told that a thousand people are going on a transport to the east.

Manus (Emanuel), Rosa and Judy's farewell letter from
Westerbork, 2 September 1944 (Anne Frank House Collection,
Amsterdam). See annotated translation overleaf.

Translation of the letter from Westerbork, page 53

Tomorrow, 3 September, we're going on a transport. We don't yet know where to, but it will be to the east. We are full of courage and still healthy and will do our best to get through it. We're in a dreadful plight here. Give our greetings and this letter to Elsje and Lammert* especially; we long to see them again and will have to fight for that. My eldest sister† and family left for Theresienstadt 5 weeks ago and Wiet for Celle.‡ They were also good; would you please tell his wife that I received her letter and that it helped us a lot. Don't send any more things to us here, we'll come and fetch them from you later. Thanks for everything. Greetings and kisses, especially to my family,
Ma, Ro, Ju

* Elsje and Lammert are code names for Rosa's sister Ella and her husband Leys, who were in hiding in Halle-Heide, a neighbourhood in the Achterhoek.
† Rosa's eldest sister was Julie Straus-Levy. She was transported from Theresienstadt to Auschwitz on 6 October 1944. She was forty-six years old when she was gassed there two days later, together with her husband Asser and their son Harry. Only their daughter Adi survived the war.
‡ Wiet was the code name for Louis, the brother of Leys. Celle is a reference to Bergen-Belsen. He was murdered there on 24 January 1945, aged forty-eight.

On a transport to the east

Nobody who hasn't experienced it can understand what this means for us. The mood was one of panic. At night the names of those who would have to go were called out. We pack the tiny bit of luggage we have accumulated. At ten o'clock on the morning of Sunday 3 September, the goods train is ready at the special Westerbork station.

Seventy-five of us are crammed close together in cattle trucks without light or air. So we go to meet our unhappy fate. We hold on tight to each other, always with the same thought: if only we can stay together. The train races onwards. Somewhere in Germany we're given bread and jam.

I have no appetite, but I'm tormented by extreme thirst. Terrible. The water has run out, the air is unbearable and then there's the anxiety. Onwards goes the train. After a few hours there's a violent jolt. We stop, the doors are thrown open and the SS shout, 'Anyone who still has gold, watches or fountain pens, hand them over! Otherwise we'll shoot you dead!' Trembling, we obey them; grinning, their caps full, they leave again. Then we move on at a furious pace; there's no certainty as to where we're going. After two days we are exhausted. Here a man dies, there an elderly lady faints, children cry – it's almost impossible to bear any longer.

At night, at about two in the morning, the train stops. We hear footsteps, talking and shouting. We call out for water and air. The doors are opened, young men in blue-and-grey prison uniforms with flat caps and big cudgels in their hands shout '*Aussteigen, schnell, schneller!*' (Out, quick, quicker!) I immediately ask them, 'Where is this place?' The answer comes in a whisper. 'Concentration camp Auschwitz in Poland. Why have you come now? The Russians are only 70 kilometres from here.' Then shouting: '*Gepäck im Waggon lassen, Leute nach vorne kommen!*' (Leave your luggage in the wagon! Everyone come to the front!) The moment we've feared has arrived. The SS officers stand in front of us with whips in their hands, big dogs next to them. Bright searchlights are pointed at us; it's like daylight. My husband glances at me sorrowfully, a look I will never forget. It's just a brief moment. He's herded away from me without a parting word.

Now that same dreaded hand tries to take my daughter from me, but I hold her tight and shout, '*Das ist meine Tochter, die gehört zu mir!*' (That's my daughter, she belongs with me!) The officer gives us a sharp glance, but says nothing, just points to the right. Fortunately we're sent to the lucky side. Those who went to the other side – older people, children with their mothers or guardians – were never seen again. They were immediately taken to the gas chamber. Several vehicles are standing ready too. We're told that anyone who has difficulty walking can go in those vehicles. Unfortunately, many people do. Nobody knows what's going to happen. They're driven straight to their deaths.

For us, the two hundred women left out of five hundred, the command is '*Alle in Fünferreihen aufstellen.*' (All line up in rows of five.) It's an order we'll often be subjected to. Under SS guard, we walk through the camp at night.

In Birkenau

It's a grim sight, the various barracks surrounded by barbed wire that has an electric current passing through it. We can make out barefooted figures and hear raucous shouts. I think that this must be a section for the insane. (Later I heard that it was a penal company.) After we've walked about four kilometres, quiet as mice, not permitted to say a word, we arrive at the so-called *Sauna*, the bathhouse).

For hours we stand there waiting for daybreak, utterly exhausted. At last it's our turn and we're called in alphabetical order. Hetty and I are under W, so we're among the last. First we have to appear at a big table with a girl sitting at it who tattoos a number on our arms. She does it with a sharp pen. I'm given the number A25250,

Hetty the next one up. After we've given our names, we have to take off all our clothes in the presence of the SS. Standing there naked, we're put in a line and have our heads shaved by Polish women who have been assigned this task. While this is happening, the SS commanders continue to walk between us with a big bulldog. We are trembling with fear, fatigue and embarrassment. We're subjected to mockery for hours on end. One of the beasts, I can't call him anything but that, rips the rags off a girl standing next to me. I signal to her to come and stand behind us. That way she can evade the peering eyes of the SS hoodlums as much as possible.

What a humiliation for us. Terrible. And this isn't the end of it. For hours yet we have to wait in line, naked. We're not allowed to keep anything, not even a photograph of our loved ones.

We're given a hot shower but have to dry as we are, no towel, and the windows of the building are all broken. Now dresses are flung at us, one finding herself with a thin summer dress, another with a woollen one. Hetty and I are truly lucky, both of us getting a woollen dress with long sleeves. I'm also fortunate enough to get a vest and undies. There aren't any stockings. Shoes, horrible things – two left or two right, one with a high heel and one low, or clogs. I happen to get shoes that fit, although they are already worn down. I don't yet know that I'll have to walk many kilometres in them, and work in them. Hunger torments us. It's late afternoon now. We look at each other and despite all our troubles we have to laugh, we look so funny in these clothes and without hair. I have just one wish: I hope my husband doesn't see us like this, because he'd be so distressed if he did.

Then we line up in rows of five again and follow each other, under guard, to workcamp BIIb in Birkenau. It's 40 by 40 kilometres in size. We see nothing but wooden barracks (called *Blöcke*, blocks) and barbed wire. We come upon thousands of women on their way to work.

They look just as ridiculous as we do, only far worse and thinner. 'Hello,' we call out quietly. 'Who are you?' They're mostly Polish or Hungarian. Then at last we arrive at *Lager* BIIb, Block 29. There are around five hundred women, most of them French, Hungarian or Polish. So around seven hundred women in one barracks. Our *Blockälteste* (barracks elder), a big fat mannish woman, receives us in a fairly friendly manner. We won't have too bad a time with her, as long as we're obedient and above all behave well at roll call. But she regrets that we won't be given anything to eat or drink for the first few days; that's to get us used to things a bit.

It's now burning hot and several of us fall to the ground in exhaustion. Thirst, thirst; my tongue has dried out. Drinking the water is forbidden because of the risk of typhus. Some can't resist the temptation and drink it anyway, but I manage to control myself, determined not to get sick. We're allowed to go inside to our beds, wide wooden cribs where eight or ten women can lie down. Hetty lies right up against me and we agree never to let go of each other. It's so big, with so many people, you could easily lose track of someone. Thinking of far-off Holland and my good husband, I fall into a deep sleep, exhausted.

What's that I can hear? I wake up with a start. *'Aufstehen, schnell, schneller, Saubande, Zählappell!'* (Get up, quickly, quicker, good-for-nothings, roll call!) The *Vertreterin*, deputizing for the *Blockälteste*, is standing next to us with a stick, beating us out of the beds. Now we're being taught what *Zählappell* means: all in a line, in rows of five behind each other, standing very still for hours. We press up against each other; it's warmer that way. I like standing behind my friend Lotte best. She's fat, has a lovely wide back and so blocks the wind. Behind me stands Hetty; it's still so cold, so early in the morning. When the sun comes up it gets warmer. Then the whistle sounds. Roll call is over.

Today we don't need to work yet. It's *Blocksperre*. *Blocksperre* means we're not allowed outside, only to the latrine, no more than twenty of us at a time, accompanied by the *Stubendienst* (girls who have privileged jobs like cleaning the barracks and handing out food, instead of outdoor duties or other heavy work). At least five hundred women can go to the toilet at the same time. Side by side, back to back. The stench is terrible there, but it will often become our hiding place when we try to get out of work.

Towards five o'clock there's *Zählappell* again, but far more severe this time. The commands in German still sound a bit strange to our ears.

The *Blockführer* himself comes to check. We stand stock still and quiet as mice. The hated SS man arrives, looks at us harshly, counts us, and if he gets the right number goes on to the next barracks. But woe betide us if the number isn't right. Then we all have to kneel, sometimes for hours, until everybody is present. Then fortunately the whistle goes, roll call is over, but we have to stay standing there while bread is handed out. Each group of four gets a loaf of army bread. Famished, we devour it and although there's a hint of camphor it tastes like cake to us. We'll soon notice, however, that camphor has been added to all our food. Still, we have to be frugal with the bread, because we need to eat it tomorrow morning as well. It's already getting dark. We go into the barracks and have to get into bed.

The next morning after roll call the command is, '*Rechts ab, zur Arbeit.*' (To the right, to work.) We walk several kilometres, accompanied by a supervisor (called a *Kapo*). In the distance we see flames blazing high out of a chimney. What might that be? Somewhere near a railway track lie bricks; each of us has to carry four of them. We walk at least four kilometres in our defective shoes. We're ordered to lay the bricks down at a house that's being built. We repeat the task three times in a row. It's almost impossible to keep it up. 'I can't go on,' I say to Hetty, who is also struggling to carry her load. But she's brave. 'Mother,' she says. 'You have to keep going. Shall I take them from you?' But I don't want that and I drag myself onwards.

'If you give up, you'll be shot dead,' the supervisor tells me. We're now going back to our *Lager*. Past us come women carrying mess tins of soup. We're terribly hungry. Back in the barracks, the *Blockälteste* picks forty women to fetch soup and coffee every day from the kitchen. They are the *Ess-commando*. They're lucky; they're excused from work and are given short coats to wear. I'm not among them, as I'm not strong enough. The soup is fetched for us and handed out in enamel bowls. Two of us eat out of one bowl, about a litre between us. It's cabbage soup, water with white cabbage. It tastes fine to us, only there's terribly little. We don't have spoons, but that doesn't matter, we take turns drinking it. The dreadful hunger is relieved a bit for the time being; we go outside and stand in front of the barracks, talking to each other.

Some Polish and Hungarian women from a different barracks come over to us. They have spoons for sale. One spoon for two slices of bread. How they get hold of them I don't know; they must have organized it somewhere. They also have rags for sale that they've taken from the sewing workshop. Hetty and I decide to save up bread so that we can buy a spoon and a piece of cloth, because we each need a bread bag and a headscarf. Our heads get so cold without hair.

This evening we were each given a bit of margarine when the bread was handed out. Wonderful.

We've been here for several days now and still don't know exactly what we're allowed to do and what not. It's strictly forbidden to go out unaccompanied onto the *Lagerstraße*, the street between the barracks. But one of us doesn't know this. She walks around there for a bit to explore. Suddenly the *Aufseherin* (the supervisor, an SS woman) is standing in front of her holding a whip and shouts that walking there is forbidden. Our Dutchwoman doesn't understand, however, and pulls a silly face. This makes the *Aufseherin* furious. She orders the woman to kneel, hits her mercilessly with the whip and kicks her until she's left lying motionless, covered in blood. Later we have to carry her to the *Ambulanz*, the clinic, where she dies of her injuries.

We slowly get used to camp life. Several of us already have diarrhoea. There is no medicine. We are weakening visibly.

It's getting colder. Lotte and I rip up a blanket and tie it around our bodies. I make a bodice out of it for Hetty too. That helps. We're happy with it. But oh no, the *Blockälteste* seems to have noticed. She checks us over carefully at roll call and finds the piece of fabric on me. I'm beaten terribly and everything is taken from me, including my new headscarf. Hetty is lucky; when her clothes are tugged loose, nothing comes to light. She's very shocked, particularly because I've been beaten. 'Mother, are you in pain?' she asks. 'Why aren't you crying?' Oh, I don't feel it. I put on a brave face. We Hollanders aren't very popular. The *Blockälteste* often curses us. *'Ihr seit ja blöde Kühe.'* (You lot are silly cows.)

The gas chamber

It was a difficult day again today, a long morning roll call in pouring rain, a march to the *Lagerplatz*, where again we stand until we're wet through. Then we have to fetch sods of grass from a meadow. On either side of the road, we see two big barracks-like buildings rising up before us, surrounded by high metal fences. SS men, heavily armed, keep watch. What could those be? On the way back we come upon a whole transport of Hungarian children, ordered to stop in front of the building. But, oh horrors, they have to undress and stand there naked in the rain until they're taken inside. The poor children think they're going into a bathhouse, but they're gassed and burned.

The gas chamber is a large room that hundreds of

people can fit into at once. It's very much like a shower room; in the ceiling are dozens of atomizers that look like shower heads, through which the gas pours into the space. The victims are told to undress, given soap and a towel and are therefore firmly convinced they'll be able to go and freshen up. But here they find death. The bodies are then burned in the crematorium. Now it's clear to me what those flames are that I see flaring day and night.

To make matters even worse, the supervisor orders us to sing a marching song. It's the most terrible thing. We shuffle sadly to our barracks.

Doctor Mengele selects for death

Every day, thousands of women are sent to Germany to work. What we want is to get out of this hell as quickly as possible.

While we're on our way to work one morning, we see a girl in a very thin dress kneeling on the cinder path with her hands raised. She has pulled the dress over her knees. That's not allowed. An SS brute sees it and mercilessly flogs her with a whip. She must kneel on her bare knees. It's almost too awful to watch. But what does it matter in this camp of horrors? When we come back from work in the evening, we see the poor child still in the same position, head further forward and deathly pale. For weeks I've been unable to get that terrible image out of my head. I never saw the girl again.

One hot afternoon there's the command, 'Quickly, at speed to Block 6, undress in the street, inside one at a time.' I think it's an assessment for a work transport and let Hetty go ahead of me. Then comes the cry 'Clothes on the right arm!' So we march in front of Doctor Mengele, the notorious mass murderer. He picks out a few thin women and makes them stand to one side. Now it's our turn. Hetty is allowed to walk on. For a moment he looks at me inquisitively. Thank God, I can go with her. Then I hear a terrible scream. A French girl, fifteen years old, is sent to the side. Her mother cries out that she wants to stay with her. An SS *Aufseherin* hits the woman in the face and says, 'Be quiet. You'll see your daughter again.' But that's a lie. The girl is burned with the others. It wasn't a transport selection but a selection for death. Hetty and I hug each other, because fortunately we've been spared that fate and we're still together. So we go on, every day that terrible roll call, poorly dressed in all weathers. Hard work, hunger and *thirst*. I catch raindrops to wet my lips, because I don't dare drink the water.

Often I hunt through the muckheaps to see if there's

anything edible to be found. I usually return to the barracks with an empty stomach and empty hands.

I find half an onion one time and, rapturously happy, I hurry to my friends with it. We eat it together like a delicacy.

Already I no longer feel strong, have constant diarrhoea and am losing a lot of weight. Today Hetty has a fever and is cold, but she has to stand outside at roll call all the same. Of course I'm very worried about her and in the evening I borrow a blanket from the *Stubendienst* (cleaners), which costs me my portion of margarine. By morning the fever has eased a little, fortunately. It's another terrible day. We have to go to the *Sauna* for delousing, where we're ordered to hand in our clothes again and stand there naked all day. There's a tremendous chattering, twelve hundred women of all nationalities together. SS commandant and SS *Aufseherin* stand between us with leather belts.

We have to kneel down naked and wait for clothes. It's already late and we still haven't had anything to eat or drink. Many women faint, but we're not allowed to pay any attention. They'll come round, if not they'll simply die.

At last clothes arrive and something is flung at each of us; they're no more than rags, and there was no underwear left. My dress is badly torn, Hetty has a rag of a summer dress on, nothing else. I weep with distress. Such a high fever the day before and now this. We have to take the blankets, which come out of the steam machine, with us as well. I throw a blanket around Hetty. We go to our *Lager* and when we arrive at the barracks it's already almost dark. Roll call. To our horror we hear that forty of us have hidden and haven't come back. As a punishment we all have to kneel: hands raised and a brick placed in our hands.

The *Blockführer* stands in front of us. '*Ja,*' he says. '*Einer für alle, alle für einen.*' (One for all and all for one.) I kneel at the front in my torn dress. He sees my naked stomach. I ask for a vest. He hits me with the whip and says scornfully, '*Scheißegal, dein nackter Bauch, kannst verrecken.*' (I don't give a shit about your naked belly, you can die.) Then he comes to stand in front of us, aiming a revolver at us. '*Ich hab Lust zu schießen.*' (I have an urge to shoot.) We have to kneel like that until deep in the night. It's terrible.

It's mid-October with a lot of rain and wind. One

morning after roll call, all the women of all the barracks have to come out onto the *Lagerstraße*. We're frightened. What does it mean this time?

There we see the *Lagerälteste* (camp elder) with the SS *Blockführer*, standing in front of a gallows from which a young girl is hanging. She tried to escape to the town of Auschwitz, was caught and then promptly hanged.

It's a terrible sight. We have to walk past and look. It's meant as a terrifying example to us.

Friday 27 October. Hetty turns sixteen. What can I give her? For two portions of bread, which I've slowly saved up, I buy a warm dress from a Polish woman who has organized it from the washroom. Hetty is happy to have it.

Selection again

On a cold and foggy Friday morning we're allowed to stay indoors after roll call. What can this mean? We sit on our beds, tense. Then suddenly the *Blockälteste* shouts agitatedly, '*Alle aufstehen, ausziehen, Kleider auf dem rechten Arm*!' (Everyone stand up, get undressed, clothes on the right arm.) The doors are strictly guarded; nobody can go outside. Very strict *Blocksperre*. Transport selection! Doctor Mengele is at the front of the barracks with his staff and we have to file past him naked. Hetty goes in front of me, I watch her go and feel glad that she's still in such good shape.

Suddenly . . . I feel a blow to my face and I'm shoved aside. I scream, 'My child! I have to go with her!' But Doctor Mengele stands in front of me, whip raised.

'*Maul halten*!' (Shut your trap.) There is a glint in his eyes. I shrink back in fright. I'm locked up with around fifty other women in the *Blockälteste*'s room, all of us very thin and weak. I walk to the little window and see Hetty leaving the barracks arm in arm with another woman, an unhappy look on her face. Will I ever see her again? I'm scared! My heart hurts at that thought. The barracks is empty, all the women are on a transport, to an unknown destination.

We, the fifty who are left, know what will happen to us. We'll give up the ghost. A terrible mood prevails, women crying and wailing. Dreadful. I'm as if frozen, unable to cry or speak.

An SS man comes in. A woman shouts, 'Now they're coming for us!' and falls down dead. But the SS man reassures us and says that in a few days from now there will be a transport for the weak women who can do light work, also in Germany. I'm now slightly reassured. Who knows, maybe we'll follow the others and I'll see Hetty again.

In the afternoon we get good soup with meat in it, but I can't swallow a thing. Back in the barracks we're allowed to lie on our beds and don't have to work.

Two days later we really do leave *Lager* BIIb, after roll call. Despite the cold wind we're very cheerful; at last we're going on a transport. Hundreds of us women walk several kilometres and arrive at the railway, but there's no train to be seen. Meanwhile it's grown dark. We lose heart . . . We get to the A-*Lager*. There we stop in front of the *Sauna*, the bathhouse. Hundreds of women are already waiting outside the building; they've come from Theresienstadt and they go ahead of us. Hours waiting in the cold yet again; it costs us pounds of the little weight we have. We stand shivering, packed close together.

In the distance we can see naked men walking. They're coming out of the hospital barracks. They have to stay outside in the Polish winter's night. The following morning most of them are lying on the ground, half or completely frozen. They're thrown into trucks by SS ruffians and driven to a crematorium, of which there are several, to be burned.

Still selection

What's going on inside is a mystery to us. At last we're pushed through the door and again I hear that terrible command: '*Ausziehen, Kleider auf dem rechten Arm.*' That tells me enough: selection. Many women go ahead of me: fat, thin, big, small, everything is swimming before my eyes. Then suddenly I'm in front of the SS man, who looks at me under the harsh lamplight, searchingly, penetratingly; a tap to my head and I'm off to one side again. A procession of women goes through. Now I'm among the rejects. I find myself wondering: have I lost so much weight already then?

We stand separately, our numbers are written down, we're hemmed in, guarded by the SS. Two women jump out of the window, throw themselves at the electric wires and die instantly. I could do the same, but I don't have the courage. Whatever happens, I'm not going to my death voluntarily.

Edith, a good acquaintance of mine, is with me.[6] She's had to relinquish two daughters, aged fifteen and eighteen. We console each other and become friends. We're preparing ourselves for the worst.

It's night. The door opens, and with some five hundred other women I'm taken to what's known as the *Krätzeblock*, or scabies block. It's a horrible barracks, surrounded by a high wall, completely closed off from the others. There's no light, so we have to search in the dark for a place to sleep. Edith and I hold on tight to each other and crawl under a blanket somewhere with another woman. We're cold and dead tired. Mice and rats run over us; the women scream and cry. It's downright unbearable. There's no way we can sleep. We all have the same thought: tomorrow our final hour will come.

Towards morning, the *Blockälteste* comes to us, hurried and nervous. She calls out some numbers, including mine. Away from here, quickly, to Block 4a. We must go to roll call there; we don't know what it means. About ten minutes later we see a truck stop in front of the *Krätzeblock* and to our horror those who remained inside it are loaded into the truck and driven to the crematorium. So we, a hundred and fifty women, are saved for the time being. We probably have the *Blockälteste* to thank for that. 4a is a *Schonungsblock*, a so-called convalescence block, meaning that we don't have to work for now. Edith and I are still together.

Weeks pass. I feel miserable. I still have diarrhoea. We have enough bread now, we can barely eat it all, but we're thirsty and there's no water. In the mornings we wash in the snow. The vermin, especially clothing lice, torment us terribly.

At night we have to relieve ourselves outside. I need the latrine about four times a night. A young woman, who has only just joined us, unfortunately misses the bucket; she's feverish and sick and is immediately beaten to death by the Polish guard. It's dreadfully cold. The electrified wire is close by. Shall I chance it? (That thought never leaves me.)

I see meat!

One morning I want to go to the washroom. I pinch a bucket from the *Stubendienst* to try to fetch water. In the washroom is a Polish woman spreading a slice of bread with thick margarine and meat. Meat? Oh, how I long for it! I stare at it with my mouth open and feel my eyes grow big. Suddenly the woman turns round and shouts, '*Was willst du, Schmuckstück?*' (What d'you want, precious?) I stutter, '*Wasser holen.*' (To fetch water.) '*Gibt kein wasser,*' she roars at me. (There is no water.) She throws me to the ground, followed by the bucket. Crying, I walk outside, where Edith is waiting for me. 'What's wrong?' 'I saw a slice of bread with meat!' I sob. 'You can imagine the effect that had on me.'

A few times a week we're given one slice of sausage, which to us, the famished, counts as a delicious treat.

One time I decide to keep it until the next day, simply so that I'll have something extra to go with my dry bread. I put it in my bread bag next to me. I wake up in the night and take it out, smell it, delicious, and put it back. When I wake up in the morning, my first thought is of the slice of sausage. I go to get it out of my bread bag but can't find it. To my horror I see that a rat has chewed a small round hole in my bread bag and taken it out. A dreadful disappointment.

Edith gets sick, with a high fever. I want her to go to the *Ambulanz*, the clinic, but there's a great fear of being gassed, because every week Doctor Mengele goes there to select women who in his view are too weak to go on living.

In spite of everything, I take Edith there. She has a 41-degree fever and is immediately admitted to the *Krankenrevier*, the hospital barracks. I feel myself getting weaker and weaker too, but I drag myself on. Our *Lager* is being emptied out; we're moved to the *Zigeunerlager* (camp for gypsies). The first few nights we sleep without blankets. It's bitingly cold. Generally speaking, it's better here than in the A-*Lager*; there's water and the barracks are lighter. I'm now in Block 12 with very few other Dutch women, among Polish, Hungarian, Italian and French women.

Meanwhile, work transports are still leaving for Germany. I was in the selection twice, but nothing – I'm now completely *arbeitsunfähig* (unfit for work). At night I can barely sleep any more. I still have diarrhoea and vomit a lot. It's freezing cold; I'm always terribly cold. But we still have to stand for hours at roll call, morning and evening. It makes me dizzy and I can barely stay on my feet. I struggle to get into bed.

I decide that tomorrow, 1 December, I'll go to the *Ambulanz*. Immediate admittance, 40-degree fever. I no longer care, no matter what happens. A nurse takes me to Block 18, known as the diarrhoea barracks.

Behind the barracks two dead women are lying in the snow. I recoil. Ah well, I think to myself. Don't be sentimental. In the washroom of the hospital barracks, I'm washed in lovely hot water by a nurse. Great. It does me so much good. I come into the ward naked and a Polish doctor, also a prisoner, examines me. Her diagnosis is: totally enfeebled, frozen feet, diarrhoea.

A nurse takes me to a bed that already has a woman lying in it. By chance she's also Dutch. We immediately feel a rapport. We talk a little. She's called Jo and I'm Ro. The first few days I still have a high fever. I sleep a lot and have no interest in my surroundings. Gradually my temperature goes down and I recognize faces from my transport. The women are very emaciated and pale. I don't know what I look like; I haven't got a mirror. I still have severe diarrhoea and it's turning into dysentery. Jo is fairly sick too, but we enjoy each other's company.

She tells me about her husband, Jos, who came to Auschwitz with her a year ago and from whom she's heard nothing. Nor has she heard from her four children, who are in hiding in Holland. I naturally tell her about Hetty and my husband. I'm immensely worried about them.

Misery all around

Jo is a strong, sweet woman and she gives me a lot of courage. When I'm restless and can't sleep, she lays her big hand on my heart and I calmly drop off. We are both very hungry and talk a lot about food, cooking the most delicious dishes in our imaginations. Many women and young girls are dying around us. They mostly die very calmly, completely exhausted. I don't want to die, I tell Jo; I'm still young and love life. But Jo is pessimistic and afraid she'll never be healthy again. The poor thing still has a high fever and terrible diarrhoea, probably stomach typhus. The doctor doesn't say anything and I'm allowed to stay in bed with her. Sister Clawa, a fat, blonde Russian nurse, is very nice to us. From time to time, she gives me an extra spoonful of soup. I'm already recovering a bit and in the evenings I sometimes stand up to move my stiff legs. Then I go over to the beds of various Dutch women, to cheer them up a little and encourage them. Thankfully it's warm in the barracks; outside it's freezing cold and thick frost flowers cover the windows. It's forty degrees below freezing and I can hear the wind rage. If only I don't have to go back to the work camp, is my plea.

One morning new patients come in. Suddenly I recognize Edith. She's come from a different infirmary. She's a mere shadow of herself. A few days later she dies, totally exhausted.

Lotte, my old friend, is in our infirmary too. She's been terribly mistreated. In the *Außenkommando* she was made to dig in the snow by the river Weichsel,[7] chased by dogs, and like so many others she couldn't keep it up.

Jo longs so terribly for potatoes. She can't eat any more bread. From the nurse I buy a cup of potato water with a few little bits of potato in it, in exchange for a portion of bread.

Now I've already been here for five weeks. Fortunately I'm still too weak to be sent back to the work camp. The doctor shows a bit of sympathy; I weigh barely seventy pounds. It's mid-January, transports are still leaving for Germany. We know nothing about the front. Are the Russians close yet?

19 January. The *Blockälteste* comes in. Those of us who can walk even a little have to get on a transport to Germany. What shall we do? We're wearing nothing but thin vests. We tear up the blankets and tie the pieces around our chests and legs. We look horrendous. Jo can't get as far as the door and I have to take her back to bed. Outside the snow is a metre high. Lines of women pass by, dressed in rags. The whole camp is being wound up.

The SS officer calls out: anyone who can't walk at least forty kilometres goes back into the barracks. I don't hesitate for long, turn round and crawl into our bed again with Jo. 'I'm staying with you, whatever happens,' I tell her. 'Ro, you have to go with them, you don't know what they've got planned for us, perhaps they'll set the whole place on fire.' But I'm determined: 'Better to die in bed than freeze to death in the snow or be shot.'

Sister Clawa has stayed too. We're amazed; after all she's strong and well dressed. But she nods cryptically at us and says, 'Stay. Think of our comrades who may be on their way.'

Late in the evening the *Lagerälteste* comes in again. She's very agitated and calls out, *'Alle Frauen müssen auf der Lagerstraße antreten!'* (All women must line up on the *Lagerstraße*.) We are very afraid. I turn over, press myself tightly against Jo and say to her resolutely, 'I'm staying with you, I'm not going with them, it's over!'

The Germans have fled

The next morning sister Clawa comes in, excited, shouting, 'The Germans have fled, anyone who wants clothes, get up! In Block 29 the storeroom is open!' We weep with joy. Jo and I embrace; we can't find any words. But now: act quickly. I jump out of bed, go outside, can barely stay on my feet I'm so weak and the road is sheer ice. But I have to. Arm in arm with a fellow prisoner, I carefully walk to Block 29. Plenty of clothes; it almost makes us crazy. Other women have already come from other barracks. Skirts, underwear and coats. I take everything that I can somehow carry. The sick will be glad of it. I wear more or less everything on top of everything else, and shoes, big walking boots with three pairs of socks in them, delightfully warm.

I return to our barracks full of pride. The women are almost mad; they tear the clothes out of my hands. I'm happy to be able to help them.

Jo says sensibly, 'We need to make sure we get something to eat. Who will look after us if the kitchen has gone?' She's so weak and feverish. Sadly, she can't get up. I'll take care of it. I go outside and see women with bread.

Some men from the men's camp are there too, sick men who stayed behind, with pale faces and big hungry eyes, and in terrible clothes. They've cut through the barbed wire and are running to the *Brotkammer*.

As best I can, I run after them. It's an El Dorado: bread, flour, semolina, macaroni, rolled oats, everything is still there. I quickly pick up an empty sack from the ground and put all kinds of things in it. But how will I get it back? It's almost too heavy for me. Nobody can help; everyone is preoccupied with themselves, one person will shove another out of the way. I drag the sack through the snow and arrive panting, almost breathless, back with Jo. She hides it all under the mattress. I go a few more times, until in the end I have ten loaves of bread. That's enough for the time being, and I can't go on, anyhow. Now I need to go to bed.

In the middle of the night, I'm woken by a strange crackling sound. I see a big fire, about a hundred metres away from us. I throw back the blanket and go outside, where some other women are already. It's the storage barracks,[8] which the Germans have set alight. As long as no sparks blow in our direction; our wooden barracks would catch fire in no time. We look fearfully at the sky, but it's a miracle: it's a flat calm, a bright, clear frosty night.

Dawn is coming and we return to our barracks reassured.

There's a lot of work to be done in the barracks. Almost all the nurses and doctors are on a transport. A Polish doctor has stayed, not wanting to leave the sinking ship. I offer her my help and she's glad of it. Now I'm busy.

The next morning I go with a small Frenchwoman, Madame Sacha, to fetch more food. Anyone who can't organize will die of hunger. We make a sled out of a chair and set off for the SS canteen.

What a shock. Masses of dead women are lying

on the *Lagerstraße*, covered in blood, frozen to the ground. They are the ones who couldn't get on the last transport. Later I spoke to women who experienced this death march and survived. The SS kept cycling past the column, they told me, urging the women to go faster. Those who stepped out of the line or couldn't keep going fast enough were promptly shot. After they'd walked about four kilometres, the SS fled and the remaining women arrived in Auschwitz, where our men were already free and welcomed them warmly.

After walking through the snow for half an hour, Madame Sacha and I arrive at the SS barracks. You can tell that the Germans fled in haste. There are uniforms on the ground. Their beds were left in disarray. Cups of coffee here, a pan with bacon there, in short: the most tremendous mess.

In the canteen other men and women are already getting themselves organized. Incredible how many delicious things are left: plenty of sugar, cans of sauerkraut, mountains of rolled oats, meat, conserves, even live fish in a tank. While we were sick with hunger, the German SS bathed in luxury.

We now eat whatever is edible, handfuls of sugar – *sugar*, which we haven't tasted in all our time of imprisonment. We're just like little children, so greedy.

We pack our sled full, as best we can. We're still so weak, but we want to take as much with us as possible, for our comrades as well as ourselves. Going back through the snow is difficult, against a biting cold wind and blizzards, but we have to keep going, and if you want to, you can do a great deal.

At last, exhausted and out of breath, we get back. But oh no! The *Blockälteste* takes our booty from us. 'It's too much for you,' she says. 'You'll eat too much and get sick.' We have to content ourselves with a bag of sugar and a bag of rolled oats. Jo is overjoyed by the sugar, it's so good for her heart. I quickly cook us some porridge.

There is a cheerful mood among us now. I feel myself getting stronger and want to do all sorts of things, but I'm still worried. How long will our food last if the Russians don't come soon? Many of our women are dying of hunger and exhaustion. I help to carry the dead away. There are so many of them. The mortuary is so full that we just tip them into the snow.

Every day, men walk over from Auschwitz to search

for their wives. Several of them are lucky enough to find each other. Nobody knows anything about my husband. He was probably put on a work transport to Germany.

27 January. It's a busy day today. Jo is in awful pain; her heart is getting weaker. I'm worried about her. Will she make it home?

The Russians,
the liberators, are here

In the middle of the night, we're woken with a start by heavy footfall. A big man with a lit candle comes in . . . Screams . . . A Russian officer! I jump out of bed and spontaneously throw my arms around his neck. He laughs. I don't understand what he's saying. The others wake up too; they laugh and cry at the same time with happiness.

The Russian looks beautiful. He's wearing a white leather jacket lined with fur and a white fur hat. He tells us he's the advance guard. The troops are on their way. I'm very excited and can't sleep for sheer happiness. Jo barely knows what's happening. She groans with pain.

I get up on time and care for the sick in my *Stube*,

my part of the barracks. At the moment, there are still fifty-two women of twelve different nationalities.

Outside there's a lot of noise; the Russians are arriving in carts pulled by small horses. We now get a lot of visits from officers and men. They shake their heads at the sight of so much suffering. We're still nothing but shadows.

The major promises us the world. 'You'll soon be out of this misery in a big hospital where you'll get good food and nice clothes.' Our joy knows no bounds, but slowly we realize that it's not going to happen at all quickly. The railway has been destroyed, there are no cars, the snow lies thick everywhere: transport is impossible. Food is now coming out of the kitchen again; Polish and Dutch cooks are at work. We're given good soup and a dessert of semolina or barley. Sometimes there's blancmange, too. I eat what I can, impossibly large portions. Most of the sick can tolerate only very small amounts.

Today a horse is shot dead next to our barracks. Men quickly arrive to flay it. I'm given the liver and quickly run away with it, taking bite after bite out of it, raw and still warm. I fry the rest in a pan. It tastes delicious to us.

For the first few days, that's how it remains. The

Russians come and go. Many Polish women head for home at their own risk. We're free, aren't we? But we Dutch have to be patient. It's still wartime and our fatherland is so far away.

Jo is dying. The good food doesn't help her any longer. Now I've got potatoes for her, as well, but sadly it's too late. With the names of her husband and children on her lips, she dies in my arms.

So my dearest friend in the camp has left me. I'm very sad, feeling nervous and weak, and I've got diarrhoea again. It's too much for me.

By chance I meet three Dutch girls, who're living in a *Blockälteste*'s room and looking after themselves. They invite me to go and live with them. It tempts me greatly; they're very cosy there, with good beds and a hot stove we can cook on. I just want to consult with the others first. It's so difficult to abandon the sick.

But the Polish Red Cross from Auschwitz will send nurses. When I'm on the point of leaving a man comes in and asks after Jo. It's her husband. He's come from Gleiwitz[9] to look for her. Oh, what sorrow. I have to give him the sad news.

Now there's nothing left to stop me. I go to Block 25,

to Beppie, Meta and Fieke. A time of wonderful rest dawns for me. I can sleep as long as I like and don't have to do anything. The girls are well organized. Beppie is very spirited, a small, slim woman with chubby pink cheeks and dark curly hair. She's our homemaker, cooking delicious food and making the tastiest dishes from just a few ingredients. Fieke, the youngest, is spoilt by us all. I love her; she reminds me of my daughter Hetty.

We feel calm here and make life as enjoyable for ourselves as we can. Polish farmers, and Russians too, come into our hut, often bringing delicious things for us, like bacon and eggs. We also fetch food every day from the kitchen.

It's 15 February. The *Lager* is being emptied out, the sick all taken in trucks to the hospital in Auschwitz. We decide to stay in our hut for the time being. We know that transport is impossible as yet and in Auschwitz we'd be among the sick, with a great danger of infection. Six Dutch women are still living in a barracks across from us, so there are ten of us left behind in huge Birkenau, the hell from which until recently we so wanted to get away. We do have contact with Auschwitz. Every week one of us goes there to find out whether there are transports, because of course we don't want to miss them. We have a pleasant time together; for now there's sufficient coal and wood, and enough to eat. There's no light, so in the evenings we sit at the open fire telling each other all about what awaits us in Holland and what we'll do when we get back. Now we can make plans, but it all turns out so differently.

It's still very cold. The famous Polish winter. It lasts so long. We fetch water each day from the pond by the kitchen. It's a real chore. First smash the ice and then scoop water out with buckets. But we're getting stronger and can do a lot.

At night we hear the boom of artillery. The front is close now. It makes me a bit nervous and I contemplate going to Auschwitz. Beppie and the others don't feel much like that yet. They say quite rightly that we'll be among crowds soon enough; for the time being we're not in Holland yet.

On 18 March the Polish police come and order us to go to Auschwitz the next day, because 50,000 German prisoners of war are about to be interned in the camp. The following morning we quickly bake some biscuits on the stove, grudgingly take our leave of our little room and set out for Auschwitz.

We take one last look at the once so hated and now deserted Birkenau, where millions of defenceless and innocent people have been tortured to death, gassed and burned by the national socialist sadists.

We leave it behind us for good.

Now we arrive in Auschwitz. This camp of martyrs still has one extraordinary torture chamber, the Experiments Block. Here hundreds of women lived who didn't have to work and who were given relatively good food. But at any moment they could be taken off to the operating table where all kinds of unimaginable experiments were performed on them. It goes without saying that hardly any of those women are left. The few who did survive are damaged for the rest of their lives.

In Auschwitz there was a separate barracks for twins, where blood tests were done on them. As an amusement for the SS commandant, there was a special barracks with Hungarian dwarves.

The gypsies who came to this camp were all immediately gassed on arrival.[10]

On a transport

A night in Auschwitz and the next morning straight on a transport to Kattowitz.[11] The four of us stay together. Kattowitz is a big industrial city that has suffered a lot during the war. After a long search we find the camp where we're supposed to stay, report to the authorities and are allocated a nice little wooden house for the ten of us Dutch women from Birkenau.

It's a companionable life here in the camp, with around eight hundred Dutch people. There are men who worked in Poland during the war, several families with children, and officers who were held as prisoners of war. We all want to travel to our fatherland as soon as possible, but it will take a while yet.

We now live freely and go into town from time

to time. It's a strange sensation for us to see well-dressed and well-groomed people. Naturally we look shabby. Some of the men are still in their striped camp uniforms. I go about in my grey men's trousers with very big, heavy boots and a coat that's far too long for me but is at least clean and not torn.

The food we get from the Russians is reasonably good although insufficient. But I manage to help myself again, secretly eating with the men and then later again, with the women.

At Easter (1 April) all the Hungarians and Dutch go on a transport to Czernowitz.[12] It's a wonderful journey, in goods wagons but with the doors open this time. There are around thirty of us in the wagon. A cheerful mood prevails. The 'train commandant' hands out bread and sugar every day, which we get from the Russians. We ride through the beautiful Polish landscape, very different from at home: delightful wild natural beauty, mountains alternating with green meadows fringed with woodland, where cattle graze. They are strikingly ugly cattle, yellowish grey in colour, rather lacking in flesh. We pass towns whose names we know well from the war reports. Most have suffered terrible damage.

Thanks to our companionship and the varied natural beauty, the journey is not boring.

After six days we arrive in Czernowitz and, packed and ready, we walk in procession through the city. Everywhere, on every street corner, there are people standing with maize bread, eggs, tea and even apples! Delicious apples! Beppie, Meta, Fieke and I each have a fat apple in our hands, and with it we go to sit on the pavement outside a bakery. A woman gives us white rolls, the first after all these years. Truly, to us it looks like a painting.

It's afternoon before we get to the barracks where we're supposed to be. But it doesn't appeal to us. Italians, Greeks, Dutch, men and women, all in together. We don't want to stay there, but we're forbidden to leave. Russians keep guard. We don't allow ourselves to be deterred, climb over a fence and are out.

It's Sunday and we go into town. Czernowitz too is badly damaged, but it's exceptionally beautiful, with hilly streets and delightful buildings. On the street we meet a woman who invites us to go and eat with her. It's quite an event to be able to eat with a family for the first time in ages, at a laid table.

We often visit this pleasant family, even sleeping there from time to time, and enjoy the family life of which we've been deprived for so long.

But one day Fieke can't come on our trips any more. She doesn't feel well, has a fever and terrible diarrhoea. The doctor can't yet diagnose what's wrong.

The next morning I go to the market, where all sorts of foodstuffs are for sale, but we don't have any roubles. So to get hold of a few of the delicacies we sell some of our clothes, each day something else. I'm designated sales representative and I sell a sweater for Meta, stockings for Beppie and my own vest, in short everything we can do without. With the roubles we buy white bread, eggs and butter. Getting food is still one of our main and favourite activities; unfortunately we know all too well what hunger means.

Fieke is very ill. In consultation with the doctor we take her to the *Landesspital* (city hospital). She has stomach typhus. (As I write this, I know nothing further of her; we had to leave her behind.)

20 April. Order: 'All Dutch on transport.' We leave in a procession in the evening, with our red, white and blue flag at the front, across town to the station,

waved off by the population. Those were fun days in Czernowitz. Many young men leave girlfriends behind, who are forced to watch them go. I too have made many friends there, and I'll always be grateful to them for their hospitality. Where our journey leads? Nobody knows. One says Odessa, another Murmansk.

We no longer hear anything about the war, but we think it's going well.

It's a fine journey, through a magnificent landscape, mountains and valleys by turns, odd little loam houses with straw roofs. They appear to be mainly farmhouses, with a remarkable number of chickens, but we see very few cows, probably as a result of the events of the war. At every station, farmers' wives, poorly dressed, stand selling eggs, or swapping them for textiles. The weather is warmer now, so we can do without some of our clothes and we barter them for eggs and white bread.

We've been travelling for eight days. It's not boring, but the lice torment me terribly. I think I can tell from the route that we're heading for Odessa. Early one morning we arrive at a large railway station and it does indeed turn out to be in Odessa. In front of the huge station are buses, to take us to our next accommodation.

We drive through the beautiful city with its magnificent buildings. Here too the violence of war has destroyed a lot. Our new home is a former sanatorium, delightfully situated in a large park close to the Black Sea.

The first requirement is delousing. Another hot shower, wonderful. There are no new outer garments, but two young Russians give us vests and knickers.

Then we are allocated a lovely big dormitory for ten women. Here too we're not permitted to leave the camp. Nearby is a camp with British prisoners-of-war from Germany. They soon come over to make friends with us. There are additional benefits to this, as we get chocolate and cigarettes from them, a luxury we haven't known for years.

After a few days, the British Red Cross takes over caring for us. From time to time, we get a marvellous parcel and every day a big slab of chocolate and twenty cigarettes. On the radio we hear reports of the situation in Holland. None too good. Starvation in the cities. However great our longing for our fatherland may be, and for those from whom we were so cruelly forced to part, we prefer to stay here, not to have to suffer hunger again. Every morning I take a walk to the sea. Sitting

IN BIRKENAU – A TESTIMONY

on a rock, I enjoy the wonderful fresh sea air, taking
in the beautiful landscape. Only then am I fully aware
of freedom, forgetting the great suffering, the great
misery inflicted on me by the worst of the worst. The
beauty of being able to enjoy being here is some small
compensation for all that we've suffered. Except that
the same thought torments me all the time: where is my
husband, my child? If only they were here with me. Will
I ever see them again? I hope; who knows . . .?

Almost all of us look fine. My weight, which was
barely seventy pounds, has already increased markedly.

From time to time, I take the tram into town. There
are no longer any shops, but in the market everything is
for sale at fantastically high prices. It's very interesting.
The next day we're taken to a different sanatorium. Here
too I can enjoy the sea and sun. I'm already very tanned.

8 May. The roar of artillery. Germany has
surrendered unconditionally. Away with the New Order;
away with the Thousand-Year Reich. The last scrap
of hope of the fanatical Nazi men for their invincible
Herrenvolk has been dashed for good. A week later a ship
is made ready that will take us to the Netherlands. Amid
the greatest joy, we nevertheless have a sense of dread

about what 'our country' will give us. In the very early morning, we leave the sanatorium and after a laborious trek through the city we reach the ship that's waiting for us in the harbour, the *Monoway*. The strict checks carried out by the Russians mean it's impossible for anyone without authorization to get on board.

The British colonel and our Dutch officers welcome us. We women look like vagabonds but are treated like ladies. Four women to a cabin, each with a bed with white sheets and white woollen blankets – it's like a dream to us. Now we feel human again for the first time. The food is delicious. The stewards smile as we sit at the table, enjoying our meals with delighted faces. The sea journey is exceptionally beautiful; I'm on deck almost all day.

A new life has opened up before us and I enjoy the beautiful face the sea presents to us. In the evenings too I love to lie in my deck chair and listen to the song of the sea, its murmuring music that goes on for ever. Shortly before Marseille I make acquaintance with seasickness. It's not at all easy, but after a few hours the sea is calm again and fortunately I feel well once more.

Very calmly, our ship enters Marseille on 27 May.

There's a tremendous reception, with a band on the quay playing the Dutch and the French national anthems. Flags are flying and an enthusiastic crowd greets us and helps with our luggage. It's moving, taking leave of the boat, but at the same time there's joy: we're on our way home.

We're taken to a large building by car. We can write letters home. Home! Is it still there? But we're full of great expectations. We're given the most wonderful filled rolls, and wine and beer in abundance.

The train to Holland

After we've been registered and given medical examinations, we're offered a delicious meal. Everything happens at speed, because at seven o'clock the train leaves for Holland.

I'll always retain an extraordinarily pleasant memory of that journey through France. At every station we're offered jugs of delicious local red wine with bread.

In Belgium too we had a pleasant reception. After spending a night in Lustin, we were examined and registered again and on 31 May we arrived in Roermond.

In Vlodrop the train stops, we all get out and go into a monastery, where yet more repatriated people come together. A transport from the Sudetenland has just arrived. I see a girl who looks familiar. She seems to know me, too. She comes over to me and cries out, 'Your daughter is here!!!'

Am I dreaming? It makes me dizzy. Did I hear right? My child here! Oh, God, yes, I feel a pair of arms around me. 'Hetty, it's you!' 'Mother, is that really you?' The miracle has occurred; I've got my daughter back. She's come from Kratzau.[13] I have the great privilege of being able to embrace her: very emaciated, but healthy. We have found each other again. Our joy is boundless, indescribable.

Many people are standing around us. I pull her out of the circle. 'Mother, how strong you are,' she says.

She's no longer interested in anyone else, because Mother is with her again. She too has suffered greatly; we'll have a lot to tell each other. No longer can any Nazis or traitors keep us apart.

'Smile, Pagliaccio'

An interview with Henriette and Marcel Salomon,
the grandchildren of Rosa de Winter-Levy,
by Ronit Palache

'Roosje wouldn't have a cup of tea ready for you, although she certainly played the role of grandmother with conviction. I think she enjoyed being a grandma. She was affectionate, forthcoming, even fun to be with, but I'd hesitate to call her warm. She covered up a kind of coldness, concealing it under all her presumed geniality.' Marcel Salomon (b. 1957), one of Rosa's two grandchildren, expresses himself thoughtfully on FaceTime. He sometimes looks away from the camera as he tries to find the right words. He lives in Germany, and consequently we see each other with a screen between us. It sometimes feels odd to discuss such intimate details of a human life digitally, with an occasional glitch in the connection, but a pleasant rapport quickly develops. He has clearly spent a long time contemplating how best to characterize Rosa de Winter-Levy, his Grandma Roosje, and he regularly returns to the words he has chosen, trying to do her justice as far as possible. He is clear and extremely painstaking in his descriptions of his grandmother, and later of his mother, as if a great deal depends on it. As of course it does, because this is her story and therefore also his.

Henriette (b. 1965), Marcel's sister, also tells me that her grandmother was not particularly tender but 'above all practical. Not a playmate granny. She was cheerful, but always with a grave undertone. A cheerful, gloomy woman, you could say.' Henriette looks moved when she talks about Grandma Roos. Full of understanding. It is an attitude that typifies all of our conversations, as does her fidgeting with her hands. I talk to her several times in person, sitting at the table in her house in Amsterdam, with its view out onto a lush garden and its well-filled, eclectic bookcases. She puts homemade raspberry tarts in front of us and pours tea with a concentrated expression. She walks through the house barefoot. She'd rather not sit in the garden to talk, since she doesn't like the thought of the neighbours being able to hear

Rosa (centre) with Fritzi and Otto Frank in Switzerland, *c.*1950
(Anne Frank House Collection, Amsterdam)

our conversations about the war. 'You could tell from Grandma Roos that she had to be strong. Even before the war interrupted her life so brutally, she'd endured a lot. I always admired that strength. She was thrown back on her own resources early on by the deaths of her parents in 1917 and 1920. She was an orphan by the time she was fifteen. Later she went through the worst things imaginable in the camp and on top of that she had to care for two, to look out for two, because she had a child with her. My mother.'

Beneath her apparent cheerfulness and charm, Rosa struggled with major depression. 'She couldn't stand it if I was in a low mood, for example,' Marcel says. 'She'd come and sit next to me on the sofa, jab me far from gently and say, "Smile, Pagliaccio", from the 1892 opera by Ruggero Leoncavallo. She was enormously keen on music, especially opera, and during her childhood in Gelsenkirchen, where she came from, she'd sung in the synagogue choir. At the dramatic climax that ends the first act, the clown sings those words in despair. I had to be joyful, on command if necessary, otherwise it would give her an unpleasant feeling and remind her too much of her own sorrows, which were present in abundance.

She processed them in her nightmares. About her time in the camp.'

He vividly recalls those bad dreams from the times when he stayed with Grandma Roosje, as he did when his parents were away skiing. They always waved the couple off from her balcony. 'Grandma was not a particularly good housewife or fond of cooking, but for me she could do no wrong on that score as she was guaranteed to make me spaghetti with sugar. One time when I was in bed I woke with a start because grandma was screaming. She shrieked, "Watch out, watch out," and she pointed up at the ceiling. "See those pipes? Gas comes out of them."'

Henriette remembers the nightmares too, from the period when she was an adolescent. Her grandmother would demonstrate how she had made furious efforts to keep her daughter Judy (Hetty in Rosa's account) with her. 'She'd quote herself saying, *"Meine Tochter, die gehört zu mir,"* (My daughter, she belongs with me.) while showing with her hands what that must have looked like. It seems she pulled my mother close to her repeatedly at the first selection. I knew from a very early age that they'd both experienced something terrible.'

Yet like her brother, Henriette enjoyed staying with Grandma Roos. 'She had a bright home on the Meander in Amstelveen. She was proud of that flat, which she'd bought for herself and where she'd lived since 1960, after a long time in postwar Apeldoorn. When I came to stay, I'd be given all sorts of little chores to do. She'd hand me a roller that you could use to "roll all the dirt away into a tin". Grandma Roos would say, "Just go and do some rolling." Her cooking was simple and practical, because patience wasn't her strong point. Her cakes were usually underbaked and she didn't waste much time talking about food. How different that was on the other side of the family. She always looked extremely well groomed, though. She wore beautiful suits and knew all about fabrics. She had been the manager of a draper's shop, after all.

'She always bought our winter coats. My mother was terribly frugal, so she liked to delegate things like that to our grandmother. In many ways they were opposites. They had a strong, obvious bond, but it wasn't a tender one. I never actually saw them embrace. Grandma Roos was sociable, had lots of friends and travelled regularly. My mother was very retiring and withdrawn. You have to remember that she was an adolescent, just turned sixteen, when the war ended. She couldn't settle into a world that was full of frivolity. She'd been forced to grow up overnight and there was hardly any room for ordinary emotions. There was no special treatment, no understanding, but a lot of pain, including grief for her father, Rosa's husband Manus, who had been murdered. My mother didn't understand why the doctor who examined her after the war had never asked her anything. People were expected simply to go on living, to rebuild, to pick up their lives again, no matter how fractured those lives were. She was by nature a person who kept to herself anyway. The war certainly didn't help.'

'My mother seems to have slept badly too,' says Marcel. 'She told me she carried on whole conversations at night. That's what those damaged people were like. You couldn't change them. My mother wasn't particularly warm or affectionate, either. She was distrustful of unfamiliar people and things, and she always found everything frightening. She and her mother might be a bit different because of everything they'd been through, we were told. And that was the end of the matter. We just had to deal with it.

'We saw each other often. One of the reasons Grandma Roosje had come to live in Amstelveen was so that we'd be close by. Her house was only two kilometres from ours. My mother and Roosje didn't have the loving bond that you might perhaps expect between two people who'd survived the hell of Auschwitz together. They couldn't hold each other tight, but neither could they let go.

'It created a certain pressure, too, that relationship. My mother went to Israel in 1951 to help her cousin and family – they had seven children – as an au pair. She loved it there and would have liked to stay. Which is understandable, since after the war the reception they were given in the Netherlands had been so unimaginably cold. Nothing would be more appealing to you then, would it, than leaving the country with all those people and the miserable circumstances they were in? It's one of life's turning points. In Apeldoorn she'd trained as a pharmacy assistant. She was just starting out in the world and didn't have a permanent relationship, so she had a real chance of being able to begin again somewhere else. But she abandoned the idea. She sometimes told me she regretted that. She said Grandma Roos had manipulated her by introducing her to the man she later married, my father. Roosje wanted to keep her close. No doubt she was fearful of losing her a second time. My mother was happy that my father, in her eyes at least, didn't have such a difficult wartime past and would rarely talk about his experiences, let alone ask her anything about hers. That suited her; she could carry on building her own wall, higher and higher. But I doubt whether she was happy in her marriage to my father. The Netherlands was an oppressive place in the fifties and sixties, and then there was the pressure from her mother. To my way of thinking, she could have been spared that suffocating situation.

'Family ties were tremendously confining. Because not only would Roosje come to visit us a lot, our other grandma was also around very often. Too often. We went on holiday with them; we divided up our Friday evenings between the two grandmas. It was as if we could never go anywhere without them, as if those people had no lives of their own. Although they definitely did – Roosje had plenty of friends, for example. But I don't remember a single evening meal without the need for a phone call. My parents never complained about it, but occasionally I would point out that it wasn't normal, the dynamic between them. I thought it was sad for my parents that they were never really able to develop circles or social lives of their own because of the pressure of having to spend all that time together. Social events always involved the grandmas. I got out of those as soon as I could. The children were expected to take care of the parents, with all their baggage. I didn't want that.'

'I think that unconsciously I looked after my parents,' says Henriette. 'Instead of the other way round, which would have been more normal. I always had the feeling that I needed to pay close attention to how my mother was doing. After all, there was something wrong with her. There came a point when I found it important to be able to live an autonomous life of my own, and perhaps studying psychology contributed to that, partly because it was a way of gaining insight into the postwar generations, with their traumatic experiences. It taught me to see in retrospect how those experiences continue to affect people, how much influence events like these have, even on subsequent generations. You can look at photographs and think, "What on earth became of all those people?" My mother wasn't keen on family trees or photos. She locked away so much of what she'd been through so deeply that when she talked about it, it was as if she was talking about someone else – that's how detached she could be from herself at such moments. But she did however regularly talk about it. In my life not a day went by without talk about the war, about small, everyday details. So in contrast to many families, the war certainly wasn't taboo in our house. She'd talk about the sadism in the camp. How people were forced to carry extremely heavy things from one place to another, how prisoners were beaten to death in front of her, or ran onto the barbed wire in despair. She regularly asked herself out loud how in heaven's name people could be so cruel.'

'They always tried to find an answer to my questions,' says Marcel. 'Because what they'd experienced preoccupied me quite a lot. But they never really got much further than saying that it was unimaginable and there were really no words for it. Grandma occasionally gave interviews, something my mother would never hear of doing. I've always had a lot of sympathy for them both, given what happened. I think several times a week about what they experienced in the camps and try to imagine what it was like, what they looked like in those days, what happened to them there. I feel really close to that family story. It may sound slightly warped, but I'm proud, in a way, that I'm part of it. What they experienced. Isn't that crazy? Part of me was actually there. In Auschwitz. When my mother told me how they were forced to do pointless work, shovelling mud onto a flatbed cart and then shovelling it off again somewhere else, I could see it so clearly in front of me. I've never claimed to be able to do what I'm describing now, truly to feel it, but I've never stopped trying. When I read everything again and see what they had to endure, it really gets under my skin. When I see someone on television running after a departing train, trying to catch it, or grabbing someone's hand, it's too much to bear. The fear of separation and abandonment makes me highly emotional. It's turned me into a certain type of person, someone with quite a lot of emotional blockages, too. It's meant that I'm not the affable guy I'd have liked to be. Sometimes I think that I ought to have broken off contact at some point, that I'd have developed better socially if I had. But I didn't.'

'I feel proud too,' says Henriette. 'But it's mainly pride in Grandma Roos's courage. Of course, I knew her story from a long time ago when I first read her diary.

It's a story that in some ways became part of my own past. It's strange that it's so well known; it's horrific but at the same time so close. I understand perfectly well that life after that . . . How can you go on living after that? And yet you do. As well as being formative, it's extremely powerful. I grew up with a lot of people who were traumatized. In the circles in which my parents and grandma moved, many people were damaged in their own way. I understood very early on that you sometimes need to look a bit further when someone acts strangely or awkwardly. To see the person as a whole. At my grandmother's parties, one friend would have been in Mengele's block, so they'd never been able to have children, and another no longer had any children because they'd been murdered. They were ordinary people with a great deal of sadness, and that made you compassionate. It's the reason why despite having a childhood shaped by the war, I've been left with a wonderful impression of my upbringing. It gave me a solid foundation, with my father being considerably more developed emotionally than my mother. And of course they shape you in a certain way, don't they, those traumas. There was always something to be cautious about, on your guard. Who was to be trusted and who wasn't? Always that quick scan that I picked up from her without realizing it, assessing whether someone is Jewish or not. If they are, then you're a little bit quicker to enter into a close relationship, or so you imagine. That's not the way I want to be, not at all, but that's how it is. Most importantly, you mustn't immediately make it obvious that you're Jewish; that too was instilled into me right from the start.

'My mother wasn't much interested in being Jewish. People from the Jewish school came to call once, but her reaction was quite fierce. She didn't think it was a good idea to have a school where all the children were Jewish, she didn't want anything to do with it. But we did go to the synagogue regularly, mainly because my father insisted on that. It created ambivalence in my mother: "If there was a God, then where was he in Auschwitz?" My father showed me which houses in our neighbourhood had been the homes of NSB members. And then there was the business of leaving, it didn't matter where to. Saying goodbye: that was a tough thing to do. When at the end of her life she wasn't doing so well and we left on a trip abroad, on a holiday for example, grandma found it harder and harder. To me that clearly had to do with the way she and her daughter had been so brutally separated. My mother told me that for her those were the first signs of what we later came to call concentration camp syndrome. I think it's also the reason why Rosa spent the last two years of her life in a psychiatric clinic in Amersfoort, called Sinai. Her fears and aversions, when she heard loud noises or shouting for instance, increasingly came to the fore. She couldn't stand it, and neither could my mother, for that matter. Rosa had an increasingly obtrusive sensation of being in the camp again. On one occasion, just before she was admitted to the clinic, I remember lying with her in bed at home when suddenly she was right back in the camp. Terrifying. She shouted that rats were running over her body and kept telling me to watch out.'

Marcel too remembers Grandma Roosje's fear and insecurity towards the end of her life. 'All of a sudden she'd get frightened when we went to the Drunense Duinen,[1] where we had a caravan at the time. As we walked over the heath, the grass tickled her legs, a feeling that evoked horrible associations, or so I imagine. I believe she'd occasionally spoken to Bastiaans,[2] but she never had proper therapy sessions. The events I've described surely suggest that her problems had been going on for some time. My mother was terrified that she, like Grandma Roosje, was going to go crazy. In her final years she often slept in Grandma's flat, so that she could look after her. Roosje had never found a new man. And she never talked about her husband, my Grandpa Manus. My mother mentioned him occasionally. She'd completely idealized him. She thought he was fantastic and recalled the times when they went to the seaside together. There are a lot of photographs of them on the beach. You see him wielding a bucket and spade, cigar in his mouth, playing with his ten-year-old daughter. That time was frozen, as it were. Roosje had a photo of the young family on the wall, a picture taken when my mother was still very small and the three of them were sitting on the veranda. That, then, is your family.'

Judy and Emanuel at the North Sea, 1938

Endnotes

Introduction

1. 'By victims, perpetrators and other people who lived through wartime occupation, ranging from schoolchildren to bakers, factory directors to housewives, people in hiding to resistance fighters and from NSB members [National Socialist movement in the Netherlands] to members of the SS who kept diaries,' to quote René Pottkamp, NIOD archivist, in a telephone conversation of 29 November 2022.

2. Conversation with René Pottkamp, NIOD archivist, on 21 and 29 November 2022.

3. From an interview with Judik (Judy) Salomon-de Winter (daughter of Rosa de Winter-Levy) by Dineke Stam on 8 November 1994 for the Anne Frank Foundation: 'So people came because after liberation we spent a few months living with my mother's sister, in Varsseveld, because we were so weak and had been through so much, to recover for a while. Then I believe my uncle asked someone at *de Gelderlander* or at Misset or some journalist or other, and he came and my mother told him her story and he wrote it down, and I think that's how it came about. It was truly hot off the press. I believe we were among the first people to do such a thing, and of course to be brave enough to publish it.'

4. During a first search of the NIOD it seemed that, as far as anyone was aware, there were three known testimonies from 1945, all of them about the camp at Vught in the Netherlands. Further research showed that there were actually more that had been published shortly after the war, in 1945. Two examples are *Deportaties* by S. van den Bergh (published by C.A.J. van Dishoeck C.V., 1945) and *Twee maal Buchenwald* by Professor G. van den Bergh and I.J. van Looi (N.V. De Arbeiderspers, 1945).

5. Archive of the Anne Frank Foundation. Dineke Stam in conversation with Judik Salomon-de Winter on 8 November 1994.

6. From the interview with Judy by the Anne Frank Foundation: 'Someone might say I was in the train with you, but I don't know. Perhaps it was a kind of self-preservation to forget that, something natural. Yes, that's possible, because if with all those terrible things you . . . And that's probably also my age, because my mother knew it all very precisely of course. You see that, don't you. Now I can say that of course because I'm old, but as a child you see it differently. Absolutely. Certainly.'

7. Archive of the Anne Frank Foundation. Dineke Stam in conversation with Judik Salomon-de Winter on 8 November 1994.

8. From the Foreword to Rosa de Winter-Levy's testimony, page 37. The NSB (Nationaal Socialistische

Beweging) was a Dutch fascist organization established in 1931 that later became a Nazi political party. The Nederlandse Landwacht was a Dutch paramilitary organization founded by the occupying German army in November 1943. Most of its members belonged to the NSB.

9. Archive of the Anne Frank Foundation. Dineke Stam in conversation with Judik Salomon-de Winter on 8 November 1994.

10. Ibid.

11. Heritage centre Achterhoek en Liemers.

12. From Rosa de Winter-Levy's testimony, p.43.

13. From *Anne Frank: Spur eines Kindes* by Ernst Schnabel, 1958. In an interview with Rosa in *Het Vrije Volk* in 1964 there is talk of a *Landwachter* who was suspected of betraying the three of them.

14. From Rosa de Winter-Levy's testimony, p.45.

15. Archive of the Anne Frank Foundation. Dineke Stam in conversation with Judik Salomon-de Winter on 8 November 1994.

16. Westerbork was set up in 1939 as a refugee camp for German and Austrian Jews, but was turned into a Nazi transit camp in 1942, when the Netherlands were under German occupation.

17. From *Spur eines Kindes* by Ernst Schnabel.

18. Ibidem.

19. From the *Achter het Nieuws* interview with Koos
    Postema, 28 July 1964, VARA.
20. The last transport from Westerbork to Auschwitz.
21. Collection of the Anne Frank House, Amsterdam. Elsje
    and Lammert were the names that Ella and Leys used in
    hiding.
22. From *Spur eines Kindes* by Ernst Schnabel.
23. From Rosa de Winter-Levy's testimony, page 89. Jo is
    one of Rosa's friends in the camp. They called each other
    'camp sisters'.
24. Archive of the Anne Frank Foundation. Dineke
    Stam in conversation with Judik Salomon-de Winter
    on 8 November 1994.
25. From *Spur eines Kindes* by Ernst Schnabel.
26. An area covering parts of Bohemia and Moravia
    with a majority ethnic German population, the
    Sudetenland was ceded to Germany after the Munich
    agreement in 1938 and restored to Czechoslovakia
    after the war.
27. *The Hidden Life of Otto Frank* by Carol Ann Lee.
28. From *Spur eines Kindes* by Ernst Schnabel.
29. Rosa mistakenly says in her interview with Koos
    Postema that it was 7 January.
30. In *Eva's Story: A Survivor's Tale by the Stepsister of Anne
    Frank*, written by Eva Schloss and Evelyn Julia Kent,
    we read that she was also keeping the food for her
    daughters. In *We Never Said Goodbye: Memories of Otto*

Frank by Ryan M. Cooper, Cooper writes that she was keeping the food for her children.

31. From *Spur eines Kindes* by Ernst Schnabel.

32. *The Hidden Life of Otto Frank* by Carol Ann Lee and *We Never Said Goodbye: Memories of Otto Frank* by Ryan M. Cooper.

33. Collection of the Anne Frank House, Amsterdam.

34. Letter dated 31 May 1945 to the Leys Levy family, Varsseveld, Collection of the Anne Frank House, Amsterdam.

35. Archive of the Anne Frank Foundation. Dineke Stam in conversation with Judik Salomon-de Winter on 8 November 1994.

36. From a letter from David to Rosa dated 9 May 1951, private archive.

37. Archive of the Anne Frank Foundation. Dineke Stam in conversation with Judik Salomon-de Winter on 8 November 1994.

38. Henriette Salomon, Henk's daughter, remembers the anecdote differently. She believes her father would not have made that move 'in a single step'.

39. *Brabants Dagblad*, 24 April 1964.

40. *Het Vrije Volk*, 23 May 1964.

41. From the *Achter het Nieuws* interview with Koos Postema, 28 July 1964, VARA.

42. According to Henriette, Rosa's granddaughter, these were not delusions. Rather, Rosa was reliving the traumas of her time in the camp.

43. Archive of the Anne Frank Foundation. Dineke Stam in conversation with Judik Salomon-de Winter on 8 November 1994.

44. Quote from Elie Wiesel, spoken at the international conference *The Legacy of Holocaust Survivors* in 2002.

In Birkenau – A Testimony

1. The NSB (Nationaal Socialistische Beweging) was a Dutch fascist organization established in 1931 that later became a Nazi political party.

2. The Nederlandse Landwacht was a Dutch paramilitary organization founded by the occupying German army in November 1943. Most of its members belonged to the NSB (see note 1).

3. The Achterhoek (meaning 'rear corner) is a region in the east of Gelderland province, near the German border.

4. The *Ordnungsdienst,* or OD, was the camp's police force. Some inmates, most of them Jews from Germany and Austria rather than the Netherlands, served as internal camp guards, responsible for maintaining order in Westerbork.

5. In the spring of 1944, Theresienstadt was 'beautified' in preparation for a visit by representatives of the International Committee of the Red Cross, and the making of a documentary film on life in this 'model camp'. Although actually part of an elaborate charade, transports to Theresienstadt were therefore deemed a 'goodwill gesture'. Among the people sent to Theresienstadt were so-called 'privileged' Jews, such as veterans of the First World I, spouses of Germans and those of high social standing.

6. Rosa's friend Edith is Edith Frank, the mother of Anne Frank. Rosa first met Edith in the Westerbork transit camp (see Introduction, page 14).

7. The Vistula, a river in Poland.

8. These storage barracks in the BIIg section of Birkenau contained the personal belongings that had been taken from the prisoners. On the night of 23 January 1945, the SS set fire to them, in an attempt to cover up their crimes and also to prevent the goods from falling into the hands of the advancing Red Army. Within the camp, the storage barracks were better known as 'Canada' – a place of wealth and plenty.

9. Gliwice, a forced labour camp in Upper Silesia (Poland).

10. Auschwitz-Birkenau was an extermination camp. The aim of these camps was to kill, on a large scale and in

an almost industrial manner, what the Nazis called *Untermenschen,* or those they deemed inferior – mainly Jews, but also Roma, Sinti, people of Slavic descent and homosexuals.

11. Katowice, Poland.
12. Chernivtsi, Ukraine
13. Chrastava, Czech Republic. The town where Judy (Hetty) had been put to work as a forced labourer in a munitions factory.

'Smile, Pagliaccio'

1. An area of forests and sand dunes in the Dutch province of North Brabant, now a national park.
2. Professor Jan Bastiaans (1917–1997), a psychiatrist and neurologist, became famous for the use of controversial LSD treatments on people who had been in concentration camps.

Also published by monoray

A Gypsy in Auschwitz by Otto Rosenberg

The stories of Roma and Sinti persecuted in Nazi Germany are all too often lost. Told with remarkable simplicity, *A Gypsy in Auschwitz* is a powerful, deeply moving and rare account of survival.

Otto Rosenberg was born in East Prussia in 1927, one of 11 siblings in a German Sinti family that settled in Berlin. He was 9 when they were taken to what became known as the Gypsy camp in Marzahn, and 15 when he was sent to Auschwitz. He was later detained in Buchenwald and Bergen-Belsen concentration camps before being freed in 1945. Otto was the only member of his immediate family, besides his mother, to survive the war.

Translated by Maisie Musgrave
Text Copyright © Familie Rosenberg 2022 © 2012 Verlag Klaus Wagenbach, Berlin
Translation Copyright © Octopus Publishing Group, 2022

Extract from
A Gypsy in Auschwitz

I was given the role of gatekeeper in my grandmother's block. Before he appointed me, Wally the block elder dealt me five blows with his cosh, saying, 'There's more where that came from if you let anyone out of here without my say-so. No one leaves during block curfew.'

Anyone who wasn't working had to stay in their block all day. That included the elderly folk, who looked after the children instead of working. They had one free hour a day, when they could go for a walk along the street that ran through the camp or scurry off somewhere to pay someone a visit.

You also had to use that time to go to the toilet, in a hut with a latrine running down the middle, and a concrete panel with spaced-out holes on top. People had to do their business sitting opposite or alongside one another, and most people were ill at any given time. It was horrendous. The women would cover their faces with a cloth, but it didn't take away from the horror of the place, which broke all my people's greatest taboos. It bore no resemblance to the normal practice of relieving yourself; it was pure torment and debasement.

All our hair was shaved off, including our pubic hair and any growing under our arms. They used the same scissors for those areas as they did for our scalp and any facial hair. It's still hard for me to talk about such things.

Later, when I was working in the sauna, I saw my grandmother there, holding the little ones against her, and I turned around quickly. I knew she would be mortified if her grandson saw her like that. There can be no greater humiliation than forcing women to go naked in front of their grown-up sons, or men before their daughters.

A gong sounded to mark the end of our free hour, and everyone was supposed to be back at barracks by that time. Those who weren't already inside and turned up late or were caught on the main street by the block leaders were harshly punished.

'Where are you from? Which block?'

Some were shot on the spot, while others were taken into their block, laid over the tile stove and beaten or whipped.

My gatekeeping duties all went fairly smoothly, until one day a woman came to me with her child and said she urgently needed to take him to the toilet.

'No,' I said, 'I can't let anyone out.'

Her husband came along and started kicking up a fuss. What can I say: I'm a human being and when someone starts pleading with me, I respond, even if I know deep down that there might be consequences. Eventually I relented: 'All right, all right, but please be careful! And if they catch you, don't tell them that I let you out!'

Guess what happened? That's right – they got caught.

'Where have you come from?'

Then the SS officer and the block elder came at me and gave me twenty blows or more with a stick. I was supposed to count along, but I couldn't keep up as those blows rained down between my hips and lower back. It was indescribably painful to lie down, sit or stand afterwards.

I kept my post as gatekeeper, but I never let anyone out again. And wouldn't you know it, the woman's husband blamed me for the incident. She had received her own beating from the block elder. I think her child may have been beaten, too, but I'm not sure.

'No,' I retorted, 'it's your fault – you told me to let you out!'

The man grabbed a hooked knife and went for me. Luckily, my cousin Oskar stepped between us, brandishing his cudgel, and beat him back. Wally, the block elder, came in at that very moment.

'What's going on, Oskar?'

Oskar told him what had happened. The block elder gave the man such a beating that he left me in peace from then on.

Oskar wielded a certain amount of control in our block. I must admit, he wasn't terribly kind to the people there; in fact, he was very tough on them. If he happened to be in the yard and saw someone make a wrong move, he would be right over there to hit them. Had Oskar survived Auschwitz, I'm certain that some people would have tracked him down and killed him. But he was my cousin, after all, and I didn't want to see him dead. I survived Auschwitz and know that I can look anyone from there straight in the eye. I never did anyone any harm. I'm just content to have got out of there.

Of course, I now had a cudgel of my own. There were times when a few people dived right into the food bucket to get out any leftovers, and I may have swung it at them.

'Get lost!'

That made them scram and gave me the chance to fill my own cup. But then I had to make myself scarce, as I knew they'd be coming back for me. I can chuckle about it now, but back then it was all deadly serious.

The people working in the kitchen used to steal a few potatoes and put them in a pot. When the block elder wasn't around, I would take the cover off the barrack stove – this was long and ran right the way through the hut, with a vent at each end – shove the pot in there, and close it up again. If the block elder had caught me, he would have hanged me for sure. But once the potatoes were cooked, I got to take some of them for myself. That was the sort of thing I got up to as a gatekeeper. It all helped me get by.

Those who were low down in the pecking order and didn't have anyone to help them would invariably die. If you got beaten, you were a marked man. The weak and emaciated, with death staring out of their sunken faces, aroused such aggression in their overseers that they were beaten all the more, until one day they dropped dead. Inmates like that didn't stand a chance. Only those who managed not to get sick and stayed strong enough to work had any prospect of survival. The slogan was 'Work makes you free', which turned into 'Extermination through labour', and that's no exaggeration. People were forced to work themselves until their bodies had nothing left to give.

The food was awful. In the morning, the room orderly would give us tea from a kettle and a quarter of a small loaf. And we were cheated even of those meagre rations: when the loaf was cut into quarters, they took a thick slice out of the middle, which became the children's bread ration. There was hardly ever any proper lunch, either, just stinging nettles and bits of cabbage floating in dishwater-like slop. You couldn't possibly nourish yourself on that.

★ ★ ★

As far as I remember, I lost my job as a gatekeeper when we were moved to a different block. I ended up working for a Pole. He was a big man named Jurek, and he spent the entire day drunk. How he managed that, I have no idea. He always had cigarettes, drink and food from the kitchen. And what food it was – meat included! When he was out, I would pilfer some of his stash. One time, he realized that his food was a bit short. He beat me up and booted me out, but that didn't put me off. I'd been beaten up so many times that it no longer acted as a deterrent.

* * *

I got sick again. This time I was covered in scabies from head to foot. There was no way I could work; I couldn't even bear to bring my fingers together, what with the itchy spots and pus. It was awful. I was treated with Mitigal, a white, milky liquid, which was hideous, too, but it made the infestation clear up eventually.

I keep coming back to a single question: why did I survive? And I simply don't have the answer. Out of my whole family, including all my siblings and everyone dear to me, not a single one stood a chance of survival. And that's in spite of the fact that my brothers were much bigger and stronger than me – I was the smallest of the lot! I can't get my head around it. People say to me, 'Hey, at least you're free now – you should be glad!' But all I can think about is my brothers and sisters, and how they were taken, and even now it's hard to find joy in this world. On festive occasions, when people gather to celebrate and families meet up, I've often retreated into myself, into my pain. It's very hard.

* * *

When Hans Koch was my block elder, I got to know a woman named Sonja. She's still alive today. I've had a couple of visits from her son, too – we played cards. Sonja was a block clerk for Koch. I got on well with her; neither of us gave the other any trouble.

'What's up, little man?' she asked. Everyone called me that because I was so small.

'Nothing. Koch kicked me out, remember? He beat me up and got me sent to the work camp. Well, the camp commander let me come back here, thank God. But now I'm in the doghouse again.'

'Oh dear. You know what, I'll ask Kapo Felix. Maybe he can find a use for you.'

Kapo Felix was in a relationship with her sister, who acted as his clerk. She was as good as her word, and Felix gave me the task of running the sauna.

The sauna was a barrack hut in the gypsy camp that was made up of a disinfection station, bathing facilities and the sauna itself. The sauna had nothing to do with losing weight – we were all scrawny enough as it was – but was there to cleanse. It had showers – real ones, not gas. I got into a good routine there and felt as though I'd found my feet again.

Everything ran like clockwork under Kapo Felix. I would get up in the morning, leave my block, go to my place of work, do my duties and return to my block once I'd finished. I worked for him right through until July 1944, when I was transferred to Buchenwald. Unfortunately, I don't know what became of him. He was a strong, burly man, but I never once saw him beat or berate anyone. I think he must have been a political prisoner.

I delivered reports and fetched things for him, including lunch, tea and coffee. All that toing and froing meant that I had the opportunity to help my three half-brothers and two half-sisters from my mother's second marriage. When I went to pick up food, I always walked past the block where they were staying. Snatching a moment together wasn't usually possible: I was always working, and by the time I'd finished for the day, it was block curfew. But after a while, I thought I'd better give it a try anyway. I went out with a pot to fetch food for the kapo, but instead of going straight back to him, I headed to the block where my half-siblings were, poured some into their bowls and then returned to the kitchen.

'The kapo would like some more.'

They gave me a second helping, no questions asked. And now that it had worked once, I did it again and again. But it was all just a drop in the ocean. My brothers and sisters were already doomed, and there was nothing I could have done to prevent it. The wailing that broke out whenever I came in and they saw me! If only I could have taken them out of there with me. It could never have happened, though – you couldn't help anyone openly, only on the sly.

When I mention my siblings in this block, I'm talking about my eldest sister, who was my father's daughter from his first marriage, my own sister Therese, who grew up with me at my grandmother's, and the five children that my mother had with her second husband. The eldest of them, Harry, was about ten. The children were tattooed, too, on the thigh. I only met my eldest half-sister, Drosla – the one who stayed with my father when I went to Berlin – when I arrived in Birkenau. By then, she was married with several children; I think her surname was Dembrowski.

We realized that we were siblings completely by chance, through talking to other people. I happened to mention my parents, word got back to her, and she came up and hugged me.

'Come here, love – I hear you're my brother!'

She stayed in Auschwitz with her husband and all of their children, and none of them made it out alive. I was glad to have met her, of course, but ultimately, I couldn't do anything to help her. We were all in a state of abject misery, and everyone had to do what they were told on pain of death. We did manage to see each other from time to time and chat about my father.

I have no idea how I managed to survive Auschwitz. To this day, I still can't fathom it. There was certainly a great deal of luck involved, but I believe there was something else, too – a protective hand held over me, shielding me from harm.

The camp overseers had a policy of tearing families apart by splitting them up. The upshot was that people would only care for themselves; there could be no more compassion, no putting others first. By the end, the father would readily eat his own child's bread.

In a concentration camp that wasn't designated a family camp, everyone hoarded what they were given because they knew it was their only chance of survival. In the camp, a piece of bread or a potato was infinitely more valuable than a 1,000-mark note – you can't eat the latter, after all. Before long, you knew to depend on every little scrap that came your way. And if you spotted a chance to snatch something extra, you simply had to summon up your courage and go for it. I got lots of beatings that way, but I'd already factored them in when I went to the kitchen and grabbed this or that – potato peelings, perhaps, or later, in Ellrich, scraps of food that the Wehrmacht had thrown away. I just shoved them into my cap and ran. If I got caught, they wrote down my number, which meant either a thrashing straight away, or my number getting called out for a punishment later.

But I didn't care; all I could think about was getting something to eat.

My sister Therese never left Auschwitz, either, but she didn't die in the gas chambers; it was her heart valve defect that killed her. She was cremated like the rest.

One time, I went to the crematorium with Kapo Felix and saw it for myself, although I wasn't supposed to be looking around, but helping to carry the round canisters containing Zyklon B. To get there, we had to go out of the gypsy camp, accompanied by SS guards, of course. We did it in two or three trips.

'Come along,' he said.

I didn't see the gas showers, but I did notice the ovens and the carts that were used to transport the bodies to the fires.

We took the canisters and returned to our camp. There I held a kind of toothed chisel against the middle of a canister and hit it with a hammer. This would break off a piece of the casing, and you could take out these little square grains, coloured turquoise or blue. A few of these were enough to delouse a whole heap of blankets and clothing.

We were all subjected to this delousing process, block by block, men and women. Actually, as far as I remember the men went first, followed by the women. Come to think of it, men and women may only have been separated later, when Kapo Felix took charge of the procedure.

At any rate, first they had to walk through a basin containing a solution that killed bacteria and fungi. Once they were inside the showering area, Kapo Felix turned on the water and everyone washed themselves. Meanwhile, their clothing was hung up on trolleys and taken away to be deloused, which meant passing it through a vapour bath. The inmates would collect them on the other side and put them back on. This was done block by block, and once the final block was finished, it would start all over again from the beginning.

I'd never seen anything like it. The lice were absolutely everywhere, in countless numbers. It wasn't a matter of scraping them into a pile by hand; you needed a shovel. Heaps of them came out in each and every delousing. If you shook a blanket, they would scatter everywhere like grains of sand. The place was teeming with them.

The sauna had been built to get on top of the situation. The camp leaders, work managers, block leaders – all SS – came here, too, and went through the process themselves. While they were showering, I had to clean their shoes or boots. They came out to find them sparkling clean. Fine and dandy. It wasn't a bad job, all things considered.

* * *

The Kanada Kommando came to the sauna, too. These people were tasked with taking people to the gas chambers to be killed and then cremating them in the ovens. They were rotated every six weeks, either because they couldn't bear to do it any longer or because knowledge of what was going on couldn't be allowed to leak out.

When the Jews arrived at Auschwitz, they didn't go straight into the camp. They were gathered on the tracks on the other side of our fence at Birkenau. There the families were sorted into mothers with children, young people and older people. They had to leave all of their suitcases and other belongings where they were. They were told that they would be taken off to shower, but most of them went straight to the gas chambers and were cremated immediately afterwards. They had no idea what was happening to them. They believed they were just going off to shower, but that stuff, the Zyklon B, was thrown in from above and then the water was turned on. When combined with the water, the chemical created a gas that killed them all.

We knew what was going on in there. Everyone did. One time, a committee came round the camp and asked the children what the ovens and chimneys back there were for – the crematoria were just a few hundred metres away. 'For baking bread,' the children replied. They were scared of being killed if they told the truth, you see.

Any newcomers who were fit to work were allocated to camps where other inmates had died or more workers were needed.

The Kanada Kommando wrenched out the teeth of the new arrivals, pulled off their rings and snatched other items. I don't know what other terrible kinds of things they did to people.

They worked closely with the SS. Some of the Jews brought gold, diamonds and money to the camp with them, not to mention the finest soaps, fragrances, lipsticks and so on. When the Kanada Kommando came to the sauna to shower and delouse, I would take their clothes and hang them in the cart for disinfection. Of course, I always rummaged through their pockets to see what I could find. I knew that when the Kommando members came out the other side of the sauna, our paths would not cross again. There would have been no comeback even if I had nicked everything they had on them, but I just took little bits and bobs that I might be able to use or swap, like biscuits. Besides, if you bit into one of those biscuits, you might well find a little ring or part of a necklace. The Jews often baked such treasures into their provisions.

The people from the Kanada Kommando got the best food, lived lavishly and slept soundly in their beds. But when their six weeks were up, they too were sent to the gas chambers. I'm not sure whether they were aware of what would happen to them, but that's what Kapo Felix told me.

He was an ethnic German, so, although he was one of the inmates, he wasn't classed as an enemy of the Third Reich, as we were. We no longer had the right to call ourselves Germans. Ethnic Germans like Felix had a lot of say in what went on; in some cases, they were actually in cahoots with the SS and ran scams. The Kanada Kommando were knee deep in it. All sorts of things came into the camp – gold, money, you name it. The finest furs were taken off Jews and given to the wives of SS officials to wear.

★ ★ ★

Camp commanders, work managers, the lot – they all came to the sauna. One of the work managers who used to come had a limp. He was a big man who walked with a cane. The children would always run up behind him, trying to get close enough to touch him, in a sort of dare.

Dr Mengele came to the sauna to shower, too. Whenever word got around that Dr Mengele was in the camp, the children would run to meet him. He would take them by the hand and walk them round behind the sauna, where the infirmary lay.

His driver – when he used one and didn't drive himself, that is – arrived in an open-topped jeep. You could see all sorts of jars nestled on the shelf at the back: big, small, tall and short. They were filled with various substances, but I couldn't say what.

When he reached the door of the infirmary,

Dr Mengele always put his white coat on before going inside.

I visited the infirmary for myself once. Some of the people in there had an incision in their skin above or below the knee, with another cut farther along, and a piece of gauze pulled through with long scissors. What that was all about I don't know. All of them had puffy faces or swollen feet. Those who went in there never came back out, that I did know. My uncle was lying inside there; his wife, too. They never returned to the camp. Nor did another uncle. All of them were finished off in there.

I cannot say for certain whether Mengele ever gave anyone a lethal injection. I wasn't there to witness it. There were rumours of it, but I don't know whether there was anything to them. He was a handsome, urbane man, and very affable – he was always laughing, never cross. If you look at photos of him, he always has a smile on his face.

Later, they started calling him the Angel of Death, as whenever you saw him you knew that death wasn't far behind. He would take a look around, call out some people's numbers and they would go with him, supposedly because of infectious diseases or for some other reason. He had a particular interest in twins. Thank God I wasn't one of those people.

As I said, he came to our sauna to shower and freshen up. I dusted down his boots and set them out ready for him. He put them on and went off to have a word with the kapo. We didn't talk in person; I was under strict instructions, like a soldier.

'Z 6084! Everything in order?'

'Yes, sir!'

That was all he ever said before leaving. Once he left some cigarettes behind on purpose. He wasn't supposed to give anything to anyone, of course. But he must have slipped something to the kapo and received something in return. The two of them were thick as thieves. It was like that with the other overseers, too. I wasn't allowed to be around while they were talking – all those conversations took place in the office, behind closed doors. In other words, I couldn't eavesdrop, but to be honest I wasn't that interested anyway. It wouldn't have made any difference.

* * *

Mengele was someone whom practically everyone had to go to at some point. At the time, I never would have believed that he had such evil intent. It was only later, after 1945, that I began to hear more about his crimes.

I knew about his experiments, that he removed organs from the inmates at the camp – everyone did. They would say, 'Oh, look, here he is again. He's back to get what he needs from us.' People just said that he took things from corpses to experiment on them. That's how we described it. We didn't call it organ removal at the time.

I firmly believe that if doctors back then had been as advanced at organ transplants as they are today, none of us would have been worked to death. Quite the opposite, in fact. They would have said, 'We don't want you around, but we're not going to get rid of you; we're just going to lock you up.' We would all have lived a life of comfort, with the finest food and drink, sporting activities galore, events to go to, and so on. In other words, they would have sustained our bodies and nurtured our inner lives, too – our mind and spirit – on the understanding that they could make use of us whenever they wanted. If they needed organs, they could just say, okay, it's that one's turn tomorrow. Then they would have had endless fresh and flawless supplies straight from an abundance of people nourished and well cared for, under constant medical supervision, with every blood group present and correct. They'd even know whose heart would be the best match for a particular recipient. It would have been the finest repository of fresh meat imaginable.

Yes, that would have been better – at least millions of people wouldn't have been gassed and burned to ashes.

I'm not sure if I would still feel completely emotionless if I were to walk past a pile of corpses today, but in Birkenau I certainly got used to it. The bodies were simply part of our day-to-day: they were there, so we had no choice but to see them. And you couldn't miss them. I didn't even feel pity; I didn't think, 'Oh, those poor people.' There were were men, women and children, all just lying there. I remember one man – I think he was a Czech Roma – who, with another man, would grab the bodies by their arms and legs and toss them into an open truck like pieces of firewood. With children's bodies, they just took them by an arm or leg and hurled them away, as though carelessly discarding a piece of rubbish. The bodies whirled round as they flew through the air, before landing in the truck with a thump.

★ ★ ★

The pile of corpses lay right next to the sauna, behind the infirmary. The dead were dragged out there and piled up, deposited, stacked high, chucked away. Higher and higher. All of them naked. By the time evening fell, the pile was always around two metres high. And every evening a truck with a trailer came to pick up the pile and drive it over to the crematorium.

In such a place, you stop feeling altogether. People were past feeling, so to speak; they were numbed. If someone had come along and put them against the wall, they wouldn't have yelled, 'No! Somebody save me!' They wouldn't have cried or screamed. They wouldn't have made a sound. Such was our plight that we would have endured anything, like lambs being led to the slaughter. That was how utterly changed we were.

In a situation like that, people lose all sense of compassion. Your only instinct is to kick, beat and steal in pursuit of some advantage that might help you survive. If, when it was all over, you really looked at those people, really scrutinized their faces like I did, you would see that they were hardly people anymore; they were more like dumb beasts. Their faces bore an expression that I simply can't describe.

The camp stripped us of any sense of right and wrong. Our minds were destroyed and our nerves so tattered that we stopped seeing anyone else at all. If an inmate saw an opportunity to strike someone dead, they would seize it; there was no longer any inner voice stopping them. You saw the same thing with the kapos and the SS. It didn't matter whether it was a man, a woman or a child; they simply smashed them over the head so that the blood spattered everywhere. Sometimes they even hit them after they were dead. We're not talking about humans anymore.

The SS abused our women. Not in the block itself, but usually behind it or elsewhere. Afterwards, they shot them. One of my own relatives was shot in the head, but the bullet passed right through. She's still alive, but she's barely there at times, and she can't bear to be reminded of what she went through back then.

Behind the sauna was a ditch filled with water, then the fence, and beyond that the cordon of guards, strung out along the tracks. One warm day, the children went into the ditch to fetch water to clean the block. One of the guards shot at them. One child was hit in the arm, and a little boy in the stomach. I saw it with my own eyes, that boy clutching his intestines. They ordered a block curfew immediately after that.

That man was tortured to death. They laid his body on a door and displayed him in the roll call yard, before carrying him around from block to block so that we could all see what would happen to anyone who tried to break out. He was a cautionary tale. Indeed, I don't think anyone made a bolt for it after that, if only for the sake of their family. There was no use, anyway. Wherever you might get to, they would catch you. We wouldn't have known where to run.

As I said, we were completely numb. There was one time, though, when we did fight back. That was when we learned that all of the Sinti were to be burned, every single one.

They had already rounded up the Russian Sinti in Block 23 and burned their bodies. The story was that they had smallpox and would have infected us. The evening it happened, a few trucks pulled up and the SS jumped out with dogs, rifles and machine guns. They set about herding the people onto the trucks. We heard screaming, barking and crashes, and peered out through the openings in the roof; there weren't really any proper windows in the barracks.

The vehicles drove off. Before long we saw flames shooting up from the crematorium chimneys and the air was full of the smell of burning human flesh. Whether those people were gassed or shot, I don't know. In Auschwitz, you stopped noticing the sound of machine-gun fire or gunshots.

I had a girlfriend in that block, named Sofie. She was the daughter of Didi, the block elder, and I had visited her just that day.

When the block elders learned that the rest of us Sinti and Roma were to suffer the same fate, they told us, 'Right, we need to be on our guard. The Camp Commander will be coming here to round us up.'

I have to give credit to Hans Koch and the other block elder, Wally, a stocky little man with blond hair, but savage all the same. He was in a relationship with a Sinti woman in the camp.

The plan was that I would be stationed on one side of the camp street, at the sauna, while my cousin Oskar – the one I went to school with – would be standing on the other. The block elders told us, 'When we signal you with our torches, run and knock on the door of every block. They already know what's going on.' If the SS had seen us, we would have been shot, but fortunately we went unnoticed. When we saw the signal we darted between the barracks, knocking on the doors, so that the block elders knew the SS were on their way. That done, we slipped back into our barracks. It wasn't long before Camp Commander Schwarzhuber and his men marched into the camp, with their machine guns and dogs on chains. He and his men walked a few blocks. We heard, 'Block elder reporting on behalf of Block 7, with 350 inmates! Nothing to report!' Schwarzhuber stopped at our block too, supposedly for a spot check on our record cards. No one came out.

We had prepared for this moment. All of us were armed with shovels, spades, hammers, pickaxes, hoes, forks and a whole arsenal of other tools that we had found about the place. Everyone thought, fine, if they want to take us out of here, then we'll sell our lives as dearly as possible. We won't just sit there for the taking. Maybe we could even get our hands on a machine gun, and then we'd stand more of a chance. The resistance was mainly made up of the block elders, the room orderlies and anyone who had any fight left in them. Lots of the block elders and kapos were in relationships with our women – some of them even had children born in the camp. They didn't want us annihilated; they were prepared to fight with us instead. This was a dangerous situation for the SS.

Schwarzhuber noticed that the lights had gone on in all the barracks, even over in the Polish and Jewish camps. The whole of Birkenau was lit up. Everyone was on the alert.

In the end, Schwarzhuber walked around a few blocks, then he and his men marched off without further ado. He evidently realized that if they went ahead, chaos would break out and people would resist. They might well have shot fifty or even a hundred of us, but what then? He knew we would have come after him, and he wouldn't have got away in one piece.

Those of us who had been living in Birkenau for a couple of years or more knew exactly what was going on. We weren't like the Jews who had just stepped off the train from different countries and set down their suitcases.

The mass extermination was called off, and we

went on living in Auschwitz until August 1944, when a transfer was arranged. All those still fit to work were to be put on a transport: 'Flex your muscles. If you've got what it takes, you're fit to work.' I was one of those selected.

I didn't want to go at first. 'I'm not leaving you, Mami,' I said.

She had a crowd of little grandchildren clinging to her; their parents were already gone.

'Come on, come with me,' I repeated.

'No, darling, you know I can't leave the little ones here alone. I just can't. They would be so scared . . . No, my sweet, I'll stay here, but you go.'

Then she herself called out, 'Orderly, there's another one here. My boy wants to go, too!' I did *not* want to go, but she kept urging me, 'Go on, get out of here!'

So I went, together with my cousin Oskar and his younger brother, Bodo. It later transpired that their father – my mother's brother Florian – and my Uncle Julius were on the transport, too. First, we were taken to the main camp at Auschwitz, where we waited. Then came the transport to Buchenwald.